# Zen

# and the

# Spiritual Exercises

# Zen
# and the
# Spiritual Exercises

*Paths of Awakening and Transformation*

Ruben L. F. Habito

ORBIS BOOKS
**Maryknoll, New York 10545**

Founded in 1970, Orbis Books endeavors to publish works that enlighten the mind, nourish the spirit, and challenge the conscience. The publishing arm of the Maryknoll Fathers and Brothers, Orbis seeks to explore the global dimensions of the Christian faith and mission, to invite dialogue with diverse cultures and religious traditions, and to serve the cause of reconciliation and peace. The books published reflect the views of their authors and do not represent the official position of the Maryknoll Society. To learn more about Maryknoll and Orbis Books, please visit our website at www.maryknollsociety.org.

---

Published by Orbis Books, Maryknoll, New York 10545-0302.
Manufactured in the United States of America.

---

Library of Congress Cataloging-in-Publication Data

Habito, Ruben L. F., 1947-
    Zen and the spiritual exercises : paths of awakening and transformation / Ruben L.F. Habito.
        pages cm
    Includes bibliographical references and index.
    ISBN 978-1-62698-046-4 (pbk.)
    1. Zen Buddhism--Relations--Chrisitanity.  2. Christianity and other religions--Zen Buddhism.  3. Spiritual life—Zen Buddhism.  4. Spiritual life--Christianity.  5. Ignatius, of Loyola, Saint, 1491-1556. Exercitia spiritualia.  I. Title.
    BQ9269.4.C5H33 2013
    294.3'4435--dc23
                                        2013011370

*For Fr. Adolfo de Nicolas, SJ,*
*Superior General of the Society of Jesus,*
*and all in his esteemed company,*
*in lifelong gratitude.*

# Contents

# Preface

Who am I? What is the point of all this? What are the meaning and purpose of my life? How may I find true inner peace? Knowing that I will someday die, how may I live my life to the full and face my death with equanimity? When these kinds of questions pop up and confront us with some urgency at whatever point we may be in our journey through life, we begin to feel ill at ease. We may try to push these questions under the rug, but they inevitably come up again to haunt us. The Spanish word *inquietud* describes this unsettling feeling that has now taken us into its grip. In paying heed to these questions that come in its wake, we may find ourselves at a major turning point in life.

Íñigo Lopez de Loyola, a thirty-year-old soldier in the army of the duke and viceroy of Navarre, must have confronted questions like these as he lay in a hospital bed recuperating from wounds incurred in battle in Pamplona, Spain, in 1521. Looking back at his life up to the point of his injury, he saw that he had only wanted to gain prestige and rise up in rank in elite society, to charm the noble ladies of the royal courts, and to seek military honor and glory more than anything else; these desires left him with a sense of hollowness and disgust. Íñigo was facing a major turning point in his life. For him the questions were framed by the context of his Christian (Roman Catholic) faith and worldview. "What is God's will for me in this life? How may I discern this divine will and live accordingly?"

Inspired by his readings of devotional books and lives of saints, he undertook rigorous ascetical and meditative practices in search of answers to his questions. The inner process he underwent gradually transformed him from the vainglorious, world-wise, and self-seeking man that he had been before his injury into a person of deep inner peace and spiritual vision, now ready and willing to give his entire life to God in service to the world. He entered formal academic studies at the University of Paris to equip himself better for service to others, taking on the name "Ignacio" (Ignatius). While there, he inspired a small band of students to gather around him, seeking his guidance in spiritual practice. Through this bonding in their shared spiritual path, together they formed the kernel of what became the Society of Jesus, also known as the Jesuits.

Reflecting on the experience of his own spiritual journey and jotting down insights in guiding others in this path, Ignatius compiled his notes and put together a small volume that came to be known as the *Spiritual Exercises*. Every Jesuit's life and spiritual vision derives from these Ignatian Exercises. An important aspect of the work of Jesuits from the time of their founding to the present is to offer guidance to others in undertaking the Exercises and to assist individuals in resolving basic questions of their own human existence, deepening their spiritual lives, and dedicating themselves more resolutely to the glory of God in service of others. Since Ignatius's time, the Spiritual Exercises have been widely received and practiced as an effective path of spiritual transformation, not only for those who join the religious order of the Jesuits, but also for members of other religious communities and laypersons as well.

Having entered the Society of Jesus in the Philippines in 1964 I had the privilege of receiving guidance in the Ignatian Spiritual Exercises from Jesuit spiritual masters,[1] beginning with a thirty-day retreat a few months after entrance into the novitiate (or "school for beginners") and continuing with an annual eight-day retreat from then on.

In 1970 I was commissioned to go to Japan to help in the work of the Jesuits there. During my second year of language school in Kamakura in the fall of 1971 my spiritual director, the late Fr. Thomas Hand, SJ, encouraged me to take up Zen practice and also become a student of Yamada Kōun Rōshi, whose center, known as San-un Zendō [Zen Hall of the Three Clouds] was auspiciously located in the same city. Since then, my own spiritual journey has involved these two traditions, Zen and the Spiritual Exercises, entwined in a long and winding road that has led me to where I am today.

In the late 1980s, as an ordained Jesuit priest I codirected a thirty-day Ignatian retreat in the Philippines for a group of seminarians preparing for ordination to the Catholic priesthood. With the agreement of the participating seminarians and their superiors, the retreat also incorporated Zen, as they also knew I had been engaged in this practice for a good number of years in Japan. Participants sat together in a hall in formal Zen mode for nine to ten hours each day, meeting with me or my codirector, Sr. Rosario Battung, for individual guidance on a daily basis. That retreat provided a setting for an interface between two powerful paths of spiritual transformation that have had a marked influence on human history and spirituality: the Spiritual Exercises of St. Ignatius and Zen Buddhism.

Sr. Rosario Battung is a member of the Religious of the Good Shepherd Congregation, and she continues her work among grassroots communities in the Philippines. She is also a Zen teacher at the Center for Oriental Spirituality in Marikina, Metro Manila, having practiced Zen for many years under the guidance of the late Zen master Yamada Kōun of Kamakura, Japan, who was then head of the Sanbō

Kyōdan. This Zen lineage incorporates *Sōtō* and *Rinzai* elements in its practice and training program.[2]

In 1989 I left the Jesuits. I am now married to Maria Reis Habito, and we have two sons, Florian and Benjamin. Currently a faculty member at Perkins School of Theology, Southern Methodist University, I also serve as guiding teacher at the Maria Kannon Zen Center community in Dallas, Texas. The intervening years have given me time to reflect on and more deeply appreciate the dynamic power in these two spiritual traditions that make me who I am today and continue to open new horizons in my life. This book lays out some of what I have learned along the way as I traversed these two paths of spiritual transformation. I can only gaze in wonder and express my profound gratitude at how they have, each in their own ways, continued to nourish and support me through the years.

In over two decades of sitting with the Maria Kannon Zen community in Dallas and also guiding Zen retreats at the Center for Action and Contemplation in New Mexico; at the Bangor Zendo in Maine; at the Osage Forest of Peace in Sand Springs, Oklahoma; in my home country, the Philippines; and in New York and elsewhere, I have been privileged to meet hundreds of individuals in the context of the one-on-one Zen encounter called *dokusan* [going alone], listening to their accounts of their state of mind and offering pointers toward deepening their spiritual practice. These earnest practitioners are my teachers, and I bow to each of them in gratitude. They have come to Zen to deepen their own spiritual paths, not finding what they seek in the traditional offerings of their synagogues or churches. Some of them continue to attend services and participate in their local congregations; some have ceased doing so altogether.

I hold these individuals, with their vastly diverse backgrounds and states of mind, in esteem and cherish them in my heart as I write the chapters of this book. In doing so I am working with a hunch that the spiritual experience and the transformative process that happened in the life of Ignatius of Loyola might be of help for them in their own path as well.

As I reread and reflect on the text of the *Spiritual Exercises (SE)*[3] that Ignatius wrote as a guidebook for others to follow, it comes home to me again and again with every page that Ignatius was formed and informed by the society and culture of his time and place: sixteenth-century Europe. In his early years—very much a man of the world, with his vainglorious ambitions and self-centered attitudes—he was also a person steeped in the European and Roman Catholic religious culture of his time. The language and format of the *SE* come out of that worldview and belief system.

Can a guidebook to the spiritual path from a late medieval to early modern European and pre–Vatican II Roman Catholic world have anything relevant and meaningful for a globalized, postmodern, post-Christian, multicultural, and multireligious twenty-first-century society?

The way in which the Spiritual Exercises have been presented and offered for guidance has evolved through the four and a half centuries since Ignatius. Since the last century, especially after the Second Vatican Council,[4] not only Jesuits but also members of different religious orders of men and women, as well as Christian laypersons, have become qualified and effective directors of the Spiritual Exercises. Many have found in the Ignatian Exercises an effective and enriching path of spiritual practice deeply rooted in Christian faith, adapted to and re-presented in accordance with more recent theological perspectives.[5]

As I recently reviewed the transcribed tapes of the talks we gave during that thirty-day Ignatian Zen retreat for the seminarians in the late 1980s, a question struck me. Can these Spiritual Exercises offered as a transformation of life—from a self-centered mode of being to one fully dedicated to the service of others—be relevant for people who do not necessarily accept the Christian worldview and belief system that serve as the underpinnings for and are taken for granted in these Exercises?

In raising this question I have in mind many individuals whom I have met in one-on-one consultation who, professing no religious belonging or explicit adherence to a particular formal belief system, are deeply engaged in Zen practice as a path of transformation. I also have in mind people who, while not fully convinced, are open to learning from and receiving spiritual treasures found in the Christian heritage. Such people are ready and willing to engage in earnest spiritual practice to help them resolve the big questions. Thus, I offer this book for anyone who is an earnest seeker interested in widening his or her horizons in the spiritual path.

This book, of course, is also offered for Christians, for whom Ignatius's guidelines may open an experience and way of life that embodies what lies at the very heart of their own faith tradition. Many books lay out the treasures to be discovered in undertaking the Spiritual Exercises of St. Ignatius. In this volume I examine the major movements of the Ignatian Exercises in a Zen light, crossing traditional religious boundaries and seeking to open those treasures to the entire world. At the same time I invite those already familiar with Zen to consider what the Ignatian Exercises may have to offer in shedding light on Zen practice as a path of transformation.

### Notes

[1] Here I express my deepest gratitude to my Jesuit spiritual directors through the years of my life in the Society of Jesus, as well as to the

many fellow Jesuits of the Philippine and Japan Provinces, and also many fellow ex-Jesuits who have journeyed with me.

[2]This Sanbō Kyōdan has now become an established Zen lineage or family of lineages that has made and continues to make its mark in both hemispheres, with communities of Zen practice located in different parts of the world. The wider stream of this particular development of Zen is often referred to as the Harada-Yasutani lineage.

[3]In referring to the path of practice taught and inspired by Ignatius, with its various phases and contours, I use the terms "Spiritual Exercises" and "the Exercises." I consulted the edition of Fr. Elder Mullan, SJ, *The Spiritual Exercises of St. Ignatius of Loyola, Translated from the Autograph* (New York: P. J. Kenedy and Sons, 1914), and I also refer to the translation by Anthony Mottola (New York: Image Books, 1964) for citations and Michael Ivens, SJ, *Understanding the Spiritual Exercises: Textbook and Handbook Commentary for Retreat Directors* (Wiltshire, UK: Cromwell Press, 1998).

[4]The Second Vatican Council, a gathering of Catholic bishops from all over the world convened by Pope John XXIII to reexamine Roman Catholic doctrine and practice, was held from 1962 to 1965 and issued authoritative decrees and proclamations that changed the course of the Roman Catholic Church, especially in its relationship to the wider global society.

[5]A good number of noted works seeking to adapt the Spiritual Exercises to the differing cultural, philosophical, and theological climates since Ignatius's day can be readily found via the Internet. One I recommend for people seeking a wider lens on Ignatius's spiritual tradition as it has been reinterpreted beyond its particular epoch and context is David Lonsdale, *Eyes to See, Ears to Hear: An Introduction to Ignatian Spirituality* (Maryknoll, NY: Orbis Books, 2000). A readable guide to Jesuit spirituality, including a description of the Spiritual Exercises that contemporary readers of all backgrounds can appreciate, is James Martin, SJ, *The Jesuit Guide to (Almost) Everything* (New York: HarperOne, 2010).

# Introduction

*Two Paths of Awakening and Transformation*

Zen comes to us historically within the Buddhist tradition as a rigorous and systematic form of meditative practice. Through this practice, one can awaken to the reality of one's true self from a deluded way of thinking and being and effect a personal transformation in one's life and vision. The Spiritual Exercises of St. Ignatius, likewise a rigorous and systematic program of meditative and contemplative practice, can be described as "a Christian system of active imagination aimed at fostering the personal transformation process in Christian life."[1] In each case, the question is, in what does this transformation consist? What are the features by which we may recognize such a transformation? A follow-up question would be as follows: Can these two paths shed light on one another in ways enriching for both?

Seen on a surface level, Zen and the Ignatian Exercises appear to be two widely different and mutually incompatible paths of spiritual practice. This point is reinforced if we examine their underlying religious worldviews, general orientations, practical prescriptions, and even the stated outcomes of each of these spiritual traditions, and take note of the stark contrasts.

Zen emerged and developed within the Buddhist family of traditions, offering a down-to-earth and no-nonsense approach, proclaiming "no reliance on words or letters"—that is, claiming no doctrinal commitment as a requirement for engagement. Zen simply lays out practical prescriptions for bodily posture, breathing, and calming the mind, inviting anyone to plunge into the practice and "see." Its central focus is on awareness in the present moment.

Beginners might come to this practice with different motivations and philosophical or theological presuppositions, but they are repeatedly told merely to set aside thoughts of any purpose or goal, and to just sit there and let their minds be still. The transformative process takes place as practitioners sit in stillness in a regular and sustained way.

In engaging in this practice, one is awakened to the dynamic reality of each present moment. In this way, an inner transformation occurs without contrivance or purposive intent. To take on sustained Zen practice is, in short, to live life on a path of awakening.[2]

The Spiritual Exercises, in contrast, having arisen in the context of a sixteenth-century Roman Catholic cultural and religious world in which Ignatius of Loyola lived and thrived, presuppose practitioners' understanding and acceptance of key Christian doctrinal terms like creation, sin, heaven and hell, the reign of God, the Trinity, incarnation, resurrection, and Holy Spirit, among others.

After laying out some preliminary considerations in a set of guidelines (called "Annotations"), the *SE* sets forth the goal of the entire enterprise (the "Principle and Foundation"), and then proceeds with clearly delineated steps toward attaining that goal. Along the way the Exercises set forth subsidiary objectives ("that which I seek," or *id quod volo* in Latin), and people embarking on this spiritual practice are given step-by-step instructions about what the mind should reflect on, how people should approach each item, and even what kind of outcome to expect. The overall desired outcome is presented right in the beginning: "seeking and discovering the Divine will regarding the disposition of one's life, thus ensuring the salvation of the soul" (the First Annotation).[3]

One way of describing the differences in Zen and the Exercises is to note that the Exercises take a left-brained, discursive, analytical, purpose-oriented, thoroughly Christian approach, while Zen is a right-brained, nondiscursive, intuitive form of Buddhist spiritual practice that is nontheistic in its approach. A closer look at the contours of the path of each of these two spiritual traditions, however, may take us beyond this surface-level contrast and reveal some mutually resonant themes.

Spiritual writers throughout the ages have referred to three stages of the mystical path to the Divine, the individual's path to the Infinite, or the path to human wholeness: purification or purgation, illumination, and union. Years of engagement with the Spiritual Exercises and Zen have allowed me a perspective by which to appreciate how these stages operate in both spiritual traditions, in a way that sheds light on each of them. I briefly summarize them here and unpack their contents in the succeeding chapters of this book.

## The Fruits of the Spiritual Exercises

The Spiritual Exercises are presented as an inward journey to be traversed in four distinctive phases of unfolding, called "weeks." The First Week opens with a declaration of the central goal. The Principle and Foundation delineates in didactic terms "the purpose of human life itself" and thus the reasons for undertaking these Exercises in the first place: to align our entire lives "*to praise, revere, and serve God our Creator and Lord on this earth and thereby attain eternal salvation.*"[4] Having clarified and declared this fundamental orientation, we move on to a series of meditations on sin—including the history of sin and the danger of hell as the consequence of a life of sin—and then zero in on our own personal sinfulness. The point of all this is to enable us to realize how far we have strayed from the purpose and goal for which we have been created, and thereby to undergo a change of heart and redirect our lives accordingly. This segment of the Exercises corresponds to the stage of purification.

The Second Week launches us into a new phase, the stage of illumination. Having resolved to cast aside our selfish and sinful ways, we are enjoined to make a profession and commitment to follow the divine will throughout our lives. The heart of the Second Week consists of contemplative exercises on the life, words, and actions of Jesus, who walked with humanity on this earth as the very incarnation (enfleshment) of divine love. In the various exercises based on passages from the four Gospels, our aspiration, repeatedly brought to the fore in the form of a prayer at the beginning of each exercise, is "that I may know You more intimately, love You more dearly, and follow You more closely."[5] As we undergo this process we naturally arrive at a greater familiarity with Gospel passages and a deeper intimacy with the person of Jesus Christ. In this part of the Exercises, we are likely to experience various kinds of "lights," that is, illuminative insights that offer glimpses of the divine presence in our lives, mediated by contemplative practice on the life of Jesus, the embodiment of divine love on earth.

The Third and Fourth Weeks take us through the passion, death, and resurrection of Jesus, with contemplative exercises based on descriptions of these events in the four Gospels and other New Testament passages. At this point the contemplative stance is no longer one of just observing but of participating in this movement from death to the newness of life in our very being. What is effected is a "death to the old self," and a new birth in the life and light of the risen Christ whereby we can exclaim, with the apostle Paul, "It is no longer I who live, but it is Christ who lives in me" (Gal. 2:20).

In this Fourth Week, we bask in the joy and glory of the new life in the risen One. The crowning point of the Spiritual Exercises, the Contemplation on Divine Love, finds its place here—the summit to which the entire program of the Exercises leads and also that from which everything flows. This contemplative exercise involves a fourfold movement and a response that thereby defines, from this point forward, our mode of being. We attentively behold and enter into the dynamic presence in four modes: "Divine self-giving, in-dwelling, acting, and self-manifesting." This Divine presence elicits This movement is followed by a response, expressed in the famous Ignatian prayer, "Take Lord and receive all my liberty, my memory, my understanding and my entire will, all that I have and possess. You gave it all to me, and now to You O Lord I return it. All is yours. Dispose of it according to Your will. Give me only Your love and your grace, for this is enough for me."[6]

Here we are ready to go forth and live only in the light of this divine love, seeking no longer our own honor and glory nor our selfish interests nor ambitions. Rather, we earnestly seek to embody this divine love in our own lives and convey it to everyone in the world. A life motivated only by love in service of others is the ultimate fruit of the Spiritual Exercises. This stage, which is meant to last an individual's entire life and beyond, is that of union.

Arrival at the third stage, however, does not mean that we have left behind the other two. All throughout, there will be ongoing purification and illumination, which also bolster and deepen the experience and activation of union: a life grounded in and flowing out of divine love. The central task in this volume is to help provide you with a better understanding and appreciation of this summit toward which the entire Spiritual Exercises is directed, and from which your life, now transformed in this love, is meant to flow in profusion. The Exercises can thus be characterized as a path of spiritual practice that awakens us from a self-centered way of life to a life sustained and empowered by love.

Seeing the entire Spiritual Exercises as a movement leading to and coming forth from the experience of divine love, we are also able to see the Zen path in greater relief, as entailing an awakening experience that leads to a transformation of our entire outlook, opening our hearts in compassion. The path can be described in a threefold movement bringing forth the "three fruits of Zen practice."[7]

## The Three Fruits of Zen Practice

The first fruit of Zen is described as a "development and deepening of the power of concentration (*samādhi*)." People who continue to engage in the practice of regular seated meditation begin to experience how the disparate and dissonant elements of their lives are gradually brought together, closer and closer to the "center"—that is, the center of their being as manifest in the here and now. The various aspects of our lives that tend to cause pain and suffering in ourselves as well as in others are seen in a clearer light.

Meditative practice provides us with the perspective to identify and name these aspects, as well as the inner strength to begin addressing them so that their dominant power in our lives is diminished. We examine this point further in later chapters, but this first Zen fruit roughly corresponds to the stage of Purification in the Exercises.

As we continue in regular Zen practice centered on seated

meditation or *zazen*, we come to experience moments of illumination that can consist of intellectual insights or the ability to see deeper connections in the day-to-day events and encounters of our lives. Such moments may also come about in a sudden and unexpected flash, accompanied by joy and exhilaration, a certain and indubitable realization of something momentous. This experience can leave us bereft of any words, except perhaps to muster a simple affirmation, "This is it!" Zen practitioners through the centuries document such moments, describing the circumstances, events, or words that trigger what is known as *kenshō*: the event/experience of "seeing into one's true nature." In bland descriptive terms, *kenshō* is the realization, in an intimate and bodily kind of way, of our nothingness as well as our interconnectedness with everything in the entire universe. This is a second fruit of Zen, which can roughly correspond to the Ignatian stage of Illumination.

The third fruit flows naturally from the second and is called "the embodiment of the peerless way," or the actualization of Zen enlightenment in our daily lives. This fruit is the Ignatian stage of Union, which takes an entire lifetime to fulfill.

This third stage is continually reinforced by the first two. In other words, we continue the process of bringing the disparate elements of our existential lives back to its center in the here and now. We also continue to receive new insights and ever deeper experiences of realization of what we have already come to know like the back of our hand. Having realized that we are intimately interconnected with everything in the universe, we are no longer held by the narrow and selfish tendencies of a selfish and deluded ego that sees the world from the perspective of "I-me-mine," but instead we live our lives in a way that is empowered by this vision and intimate realization of interconnectedness with all. This vision flows naturally into a life characterized by compassion. The unfolding of this vision and realization in our day-to-day lives, in our attitudes and words, in the concrete decisions and actions involved, and in the way we relate to everyone else—is the "embodiment of the peerless way," that is, a way of life empowered by love and compassion for all beings.

Some schools of Zen, such as the Rinzai or the Harada-Yasutani lineages, tend to focus attention on and give utmost importance to the second fruit, crystallized in a sudden breakthrough (kenshō) experience that is said to mark a definitive change in individual practitioners' views of themselves, the world, and reality as a whole. Other schools, including the Japanese-based Sōtō tradition as well as some Chinese-, Korean-, and Vietnamese-based lineages, place more emphasis on the third fruit—the embodiment of the Zen way in our day-to-day lives, centered on the practice of mindfulness that gradually moves us toward the deepening of wisdom and compassion.[8]

In sum, considering the three stages of the human path to the infinite—to human wholeness—Zen and the Ignatian Spiritual Exercises manifest movements and themes that may be understood and appreciated better in a mutual light. What can those who undertake the Spiritual Exercises learn from Zen practice in a way that may enhance and enrich their experience and appreciation of the Exercises? Conversely, what can Zen practitioners learn from the Exercises in a way that enhances their Zen path? Keeping these two questions in mind, let's walk together through the key movements of the Spiritual Exercises, gaining some perspectives and insights deriving from Zen tradition and practice along the way.

## Notes

[1] See Ken Becker, *Unlikely Companions: C. G. Jung on the Spiritual Exercises of Ignatius of Loyola* (Surrey, UK: Inigo Enterprises, 2001), 51.

[2] See Shunryu Suzuki, *Zen Mind, Beginner's Mind* (NY: Weatherhill, 1999) for an eloquently simple presentation of key Zen themes.

[3] Anthony Mottola, *The Spiritual Exercises of St. Ignatius Loyola*, intro. Robert Gleason, SJ (New York: Image Books, 1964), 37.

[4] My revised translation of this important phrase in the Principle and Foundation. See ibid., 47, for a different version.

[5] Ignatius's text reads, "Here I will ask for an intimate knowledge of the Lord, that I may love and follow him better" (ibid., 69).

[6] This prayer is called *Suscipe*, the Latin for "Take and receive." See ibid., 104 (lightly adapted).

[7] These have been referred to as "three aims of Zen" in Philip Kapleau, ed., *The Three Pillars of Zen*, rev. and exp. ed. (New York: Anchor Books, 1980), 49–52. Avoiding the language of "means and end," or "purpose/goal," I prefer to refer to these as the "three fruits" of Zen practice. See R. Habito, *Healing Breath: Zen for Christians and Buddhists in a Wounded World* (Boston: Wisdom Publications, 2006), chaps. 3 and 4.

[8] The debate between "sudden" and "gradual" awakening has been going on within the Zen tradition for centuries and continues to be an implicit or explicit feature in characterizing the particular style of various lineages.

# PART ONE

# *PREPARING THE WAY*

We prepare to launch our inward journey by taking stock of our resources, looking at maps drawn by others who have undertaken the journey before us, and ascertaining our destination. The first three chapters will address these items involved in the preparation.

Chapter 1 will examine key terms in the theological vocabulary used by Ignatius of Loyola, exploring ways wherein spiritual seekers from different religious traditions or of no particular religious background may connect with his message and follow him on his path. It will also present key features of the Zen path, inviting seekers, including those to some extent already familiar with the Spiritual Exercises, to take it on for themselves. Chapter 2 will consider the preparatory notes laid down by Ignatius in his Spiritual Exercises, highlighting some particular points to bear in mind in undertaking the inward journey, also noting points of comparison and contrast with the Zen path. Chapter 3 addresses the ultimate destination of the inward journey, considering the Principle and Foundation as laid down by Ignatius on the one hand, and the underlying motivation that propels those engaged in Zen practice on the other.

*This is no other than to resolve the big questions of human existence: Who am I? Why am I here?*

*The succeeding chapters will then explore the contours of the stages of Purification (Chapters 4 and 5), Illumination (Chapters 6 to 9), and Union (Chapters 10 to 12).*

# 1

# Translating Ignatius, Presenting Zen

The *Spiritual Exercises of St. Ignatius* has its distinctive place among the religious classics that continue to influence human culture across historical and geographical boundaries. Highlighting the lasting significance of such works that belong in this category, theologian David Tracy suggests, "Though highly particular in origin and expression, classics have the possibility of being universal in their effect."[1]

In this volume I take up the religious classic called the *Spiritual Exercises of St. Ignatius* to explore what can be of enduring significance for us in our twenty-first-century multireligious global culture. Our project, in short, entails translating Ignatius.

The word "translate" comes from the Latin, meaning "to carry across" or to "bring over." In this book I want to take Ignatius and carry him over and listen to what he might have to say to people of a different epoch, culture, and religious context. In other words, we must carry Ignatius's message as enshrined in his Spiritual Exercises across and beyond its origins in late medieval to early modern European culture and society, rendering key expressions embedded in the worldview of Roman Catholicism of that time in ways that spiritual seekers across religious traditions and in a modern era may access.

Our task is like that of a linguistic interpreter, a "translator" in the common usage of the word. A translator's work is not simply converting the words and sentences of one language into another. Equipped with an understanding and appreciation of the language as well as the context and culture of the speaker, a translator who is able to carry out the task effectively is also familiar with the language, context, and culture of the listener for whom the translation is being rendered. An adept translator presents the message from within the structures and nuanced meanings of the new language.

Translating Ignatius and his spiritual legacy into different cultures and contexts has been an ongoing task of his followers through the centuries.[2] A notable and recently published volume in this vein is Roger Haight's *Christian Spirituality for Seekers: Reflections on the Spiritual Exercises of Ignatius Loyola*, written for "a broad audience, not excluding Catholics but more pointedly addressing Protestants and also people outside Christianity, perhaps members of other religions, perhaps with no religious affiliation, who are looking for spiritual depth."[3]

In this vein I present this volume to seekers of different backgrounds and religious (or no religious) affiliation who, perhaps somewhat curious about this renowned spiritual classic, might wish to check out what's in it for them. I have in mind specifically those who are exploring spiritual paths, who may or may not already be engaged in Zen or some form of meditation, whether Buddhist, Hindu, Jewish, Muslim, or Christian, or from some other tradition. I am working with the hunch that, notwithstanding apparent and rather obvious differences, they may find a kindred spirit in Ignatius of Loyola.

This volume is also for people who are already familiar in varying degrees with the Spiritual Exercises, including people who direct others in Ignatian retreats and who have undertaken such retreats under the guidance of a spiritual director. As such people explore the various contours of the Ignatian Exercises from a Zen perspective, my hope is that they may be able to see already familiar territory in a new and even fresher light.

In translating Ignatius, we need to take a look at key terms frequently used in the Spiritual Exercises that can serve as immediate roadblocks to people coming from outside the Christian tradition. We consider these terms and reflect upon them, listening to the deeper levels of resonance in our human experience in a way that may shed new light on their significance and enable us to go beyond religious as well as ideological and other boundaries that separate our human community.

## God

The term "God our Creator and Lord" occurs repeatedly throughout the Exercises. Ignatius's formulation of the why and wherefore of our life on earth, called the Principle and Foundation and presented right at the opening of the Exercises, hinges on this central term, upon which the entire enterprise of human life is grounded and oriented. The opening line reads: "We human beings are created to praise, reverence, and serve God our Creator and Lord, and in so doing, attain our eternal salvation." People from a monotheistic religious background may have a fairly well-defined understanding of this term as used in their respective religious communities. Adherents can simply refer to the basic tenets of their own religious tradition for an elucidation of the term's meaning and content. Devout followers of the Abrahamic traditions (Jewish, Christian, or Muslim) may thus readily be able to accept Ignatius's statement of the Principle and Foundation as they embark on their spiritual journey. Putatively, the same may be said about people from the Vishistadvaitic school of the Hindu tradition (following the thought of the medieval Indian sage Rāmānuja), and from other forms of monotheistic belief systems whose view of ultimate reality centers on a personal God as the ground and goal of human existence.

Following Ignatius's guidance, people grounded in such traditions can go on to the next stages of the path with a clear sense of direction based on this opening statement. But even, or perhaps especially, for such persons, I would like to offer some suggestions before moving on to the next step of the Exercises, keeping in mind that other people may not be ready to go forward pending further elucidation of Ignatius's theological language.

Many earnest seekers, some of whom may already be engaged in some form of meditative or spiritual practice, find God-language problematic from the start and thus face a stumbling block right at the gateway of the Ignatian Exercises.

For one thing, the image of God in the minds of many devout Jewish, Christian, and Muslim followers as an Almighty Being who rewards the good and punishes the wicked can be troublesome. This God is judgmental and even vengeful, behaving in unpredictable or even capricious ways—answering some prayers and not others, favoring some people and ignoring others. This God may leave an earnest seeker cold, asking how a person could "praise, reverence, and serve" such a being.

When our younger son, Benjamin, was a freshman at a Jesuit-run university in the Northeast, he came home after his first semester for Christmas break declaring, "I don't believe in God anymore." When asked why, he described what he learned about God from a theology course, which happened to be an introduction to the Old Testament. What he learned about the image of God seen from the historical experience of the people of Israel was that of a male tribal deity—mighty and protective of his people against their enemies (the Egyptians, the surrounding tribes in the desert areas around them), but also capricious, vengeful, and manifesting what psychologists might call Borderline Personality Disorder in his relationship with his chosen people. Benjamin would have no more of this God.

Further, God-language in the public arena today is associated with certain kinds of groups with political motives that divide our human community along religious, theological, or ideological lines. Such groups push for legislation that would exclude or discriminate against segments of the population based on gender or sexual orientation, in a way that puts off even many sincere religious believers. Then there is the ongoing influence of the anti-God discourse popularized by militant atheist writers who cite the familiar arguments about how religion, specifically belief in a monotheistic deity, is, as Karl Marx famously stated, an "opiate of the people." Throughout history theistic religion has been a motivation for destructive and violent activity by human beings, each group proclaiming, "God is on our side!"

While devout believers may not be swayed into abandoning their religious faith altogether, they also need to pay heed to such voices and be able to take a self-critical stance on the way they live their faith. Religious adherents also need to take to task their own communities, examining them for attitudes and behavior that lead in the direction of exclusivist, judgmental, and holier-than thou stances toward others.

A more unwieldy problem connected with using God-language in the context of launching a spiritual path is that the term "God" itself carries so much historical, sociological, and doctrinal and institutional baggage that tends to get in the way of authentic spiritual experience.[4] In other words, especially referring to those who profess adherence to a monotheistic belief system, an idea of God or God our Creator and Lord may already be embedded deep in our psyche as a conceptual belief that we hold on to, with visual imagery, lists of attributes, and so on. This mind-set can present an obstacle to expanding our horizons through an experiential encounter with that which is yet unknown.

A genuine spiritual experience may call upon us to let go of the God images that have formed in our minds since childhood, notably that of the grandfather in the sky with a long white beard watching over us, rewarding us when we are good and punishing us when we are bad. Starkly put, such an image of God must die in order for a living and transformative encounter with Mystery to take place. Even graced with such an experiential encounter that we are able to acknowledge and recognize from within the intimate recesses of our being, we are still left largely in the realm of the unknown.[5]

How, then, is an earnest seeker who is skeptical or somewhat hesitant about the use of God-language, though remaining open to an experiential encounter with Mystery, to approach the Spiritual Exercises of St. Ignatius, teeming as it does throughout the entire program with expressions referring to "God," "God our Creator and Lord," and its many variations?

As we proceed through the Ignatian Exercises, I would like to suggest that we set aside as much as possible any conceptual content that people tend to associate with the term "God," including such tradition-bound and mind-boggling terms as "almighty," "all-knowing," "absolute," "sovereign," and "supreme being." Each of these notions presents its own set of conceptual problems that need to be unpacked so that we are not hindered in our inward journey. For people who have already made up their minds that all God-language is meaningless nonsense, I have nothing to offer except to recommend a book by philosopher Gerald Benedict titled *The God Debate*, which examines the issues involved in the question about God's "existence" and untangles some of the conceptual cobwebs associated with this term.[6]

In this regard, allow me to offer a way of reframing an approach to the God-language in Ignatius's usage. I take my cue from Norman Fischer, poet, Zen master, and former abbot of the San Francisco Zen Center. In the introductory chapter to his book *Opening to You: Zen-Inspired Translations of the Psalms*, he writes,

> For some years I had been giving thought to the question of who the audience of my poetry actually was. I came to see that I was not writing for ordinary persons, not for colleagues, not for poetry lovers. The person to whom my poems actually seemed to be addressed was someone much more silent and much more profoundly receptive than any human being could possibly be. This person wasn't a person at all. It was nobody, nothing, and it wasn't anywhere or at anytime. It was even beyond meaning. So poetry is important to me not because it gives me a chance to express myself, or to communicate, but because it is an encounter with that which is both so close to me I can't see it and so far away I can never reach it.[7]

From this description, we can see that Fischer is accountable to that "someone" so intimately close and yet beyond reach, to that silent audience receptive to the poetry that will emerge, as if expecting no less than the best insofar as his craft as a poet is concerned. The awareness of that someone so profoundly receptive to what a poet has to offer, and thereby so expectant of the poet's best, is what empowers and inspires the poet precisely to come forth with nothing less than the best, also preventing the poet from slackening or being satisfied with mediocre work.

Following Fischer, I suggest that we as human beings, each in our own deeply personal and intimate ways, are called to an encounter with that which is both so close to us that we can't see it and so far away that we can never reach it. We do not need to name it for the moment; we do not offer proofs of its existence, nor a conceptual definition of what it is, but we simply offer it as an invitation to the earnest seeker to consider for now as a horizon of awareness. As the poet is accountable to and at the same time empowered and inspired by that (unknown) someone to offer the best of his or her poetic craft, we human beings, living our lives and making our individual choices in the course of that life, are accountable and responsible—that is, response-able—to an unknown someone who empowers us and inspires us to be the best we can be and to live our best life.

Even using the terms "that" or "someone" to refer to this horizon, we also need to be cautious of our language's limitations when it comes to this dimension. We are not referring to an objective reality here, nor to a subjective reality. It is neither object nor subject, but precisely a horizon of awareness that springs forth from and resonates within the deepest recesses of our own being. As St. Augustine described it, it is "more intimate to me than I am to myself" (*Confessions* III, 6:11). It is also so far beyond all that we can ever conceive or imagine that it is "wholly Other," as Karl Barth and many other theologians point out.

Is there a way of using the name "God" that is meaningful for adherents of monotheistic religious traditions as well as for people who regard themselves as agnostic or noncommitted? Fischer's term for the poet's unseen audience—the horizon of awareness—may be taken as applying to all earnest seekers open to an encounter with the unknown as they pursue a spiritual path.

## Jesus Christ

Another central term that undergirds the Exercises is "Jesus Christ our Lord" or "Christ our Lord." In using this term, Ignatius affirms a fundamental doctrine that is the keystone and hallmark of the entire Christian tradition: Jesus Christ is the Second Person of the Triune God, who came down to earth, crossing the unbridgeable chasm between the human and the Divine. A passage from John's Gospel conveys this doctrinal stance: "God so loved the world that he gave his only Son" (John 3:16).

Ignatius read the Gospels and understood all the words and actions of Jesus as those of the Incarnate Word who was with God from the beginning (John 1:1–18), the Anointed One (Christ) who came to show us human beings the way back to God from our sinful, alienated state of being.

We need to take a step back at this point to apply a wider-angle lens, asking a question that brings us across religious boundaries: "Who is Jesus Christ?"

Since the nineteenth century several waves of study have occurred in what has been called the "quest for the historical Jesus" or the search for the "Jesus of history." In this field, scholars attempt to sift through the New Testament writings to piece together something resembling a biography of Jesus; such a depiction would also distinguish Jesus from the "Christ of faith." Of late, a group of scholars belonging to what is called "the Jesus seminar" have provided valuable insights on this matter. But in the wake of all this activity, causing us to be a little more cautious about our statements of "what Jesus was really like," we are still left in the dark about who the historical Jesus was.

The community of followers that emerged after the death of Jesus gradually won more and more adherents in the surrounding areas of Palestine and beyond, later becoming the dominant spiritual power in the Roman Empire. Centuries of debate and wrangling took place among the followers of Jesus to come to a consensus on how to properly define in human language who Jesus was for them—and is today. In the course of these debates in the first four centuries after Jesus' death, many such attempts were eventually discounted and dismissed as heresy.

In 325 CE, a council of the bishops who were successors of the original twelve apostles was held at Nicaea, a city in the Roman Empire. This assembly came out with a proclamation—referred to as the Nicene Creed, after the city in which it was held—that expressed the general consensus that the council reached. This statement of Christian doctrine has now become the normative expression of what Christians believe about God, Jesus Christ, the Holy Spirit, the church, and eternal salvation. It is still recited aloud at worship in churches throughout the world.

According to this creedal statement, Jesus is the Incarnate Son of God, the Second Person of the Trinity, who came to earth to reveal to us fallen human beings the Way back to God the Father. Jesus is now "seated at the right hand of the Father . . . and will come again to judge the living and the dead."

For people of other religious traditions who look at Jesus with a favorable disposition, he is variously described as an enlightened teacher (Buddhism), a divine manifestation or avatar (Hinduism), a prophet (Islam), or an itinerant rabbi (Judaism).[8] For others less favorably disposed, Jesus was a sorcerer, a magician or trickster, or a charlatan who misled the multitudes. Even worse, he is cited as the cause of much religious intolerance, bigotry, and violence that his followers throughout history wrought on those who believed differently, using political, military, and other forms of power. Given the profound impact Jesus has made on human history during the past two millennia and the passionate debates that have been and continue to be elicited as his name is brought up, writing about Jesus in a dispassionate way is not possible.[9]

In the Spiritual Exercises, Jesus is presented as the central subject of contemplative practice in the Second, Third, and Fourth Weeks. Ignatius assumed that those who would take up the Exercises would have the same understanding regarding the identity and the foundational place of Jesus in Christian life and spirituality, and so it has been with the vast majority of people who have undertaken this path of spiritual practice. Countless persons throughout the more than four and a half centuries that the Exercises have been offered since Ignatius have found in them the transformation and empowerment for a new life in freedom that they were looking for, in selfless service to God and the world following in the spirit of Jesus Christ.

The question for us here is whether a spiritual seeker who may not share the traditional Christian understanding about nor profess belief in Jesus as the Incarnate Son of God, the Second Person of the Trinity, and so on, can proceed from this point. Can non-Christians undertake the Ignatian Exercises in a way that leads them to the spiritual transformation that the Exercises intend?

I offer a suggestion in this regard, which is not meant to deny or discount the traditional Christian understanding but is suggested as one approach that might open the Ignatian Exercises to a wider group beyond the Christian fold. I address this point in a roundabout way, looking at how Zen practitioners are given guidance in realizing the Way and embodying it in their own lives.

In Zen, a person who comes to a teacher for guidance with questions such as "Who am I? What is my ultimate destiny? What is the point of all this?" is often given a practice device (called a "koan") as a way of providing directions for deepening his or her practice and coming to a transformative experience. The word "koan" comes from a Chinese/Japanese character compound, literally meaning "public case," which is a presentation of a verbal exchange or description of an encounter between a Zen master and a student, or between two or more Zen adepts. One koan found effective in this regard is the well-known koan "Mu": "A monk asked the Master, 'Does a dog have Buddha nature?' The Master said, 'Mu!'"

After being told about the exchange between the monk and the Zen master, practitioners are then advised to set aside the monk, the Zen master, the dog, and Buddha nature altogether, and just let their minds, hearts, and entire being focus on this opaque, impenetrable, mind-stopping syllable that is Mu. As they sit in stillness, they are advised to let this silent sound of Mu accompany their out-breath repeatedly.[10]

Mu is not to be taken as having any conceptual content, nor is it a secret word whose meaning is to be discovered in the practice of Zen meditation. Rather, Mu can be taken as a placeholder for and pointer to that which is beyond words or concepts, a realm that opens up with the stilling of the discursive mind. Practitioners are invited to plunge more deeply into Mu in such a way that the line separating the practitioner from Mu gradually melts away.

After students engage in the practice of Mu for a given time, the teacher asks each student in the one-to-one encounter of dokusan, "What is Mu?" The teacher may also say, Show me Mu!" The teacher is not looking for a definition of Mu. Instead, the question is meant to be like a doctor's rubber mallet, tapping on a knee to check whether a reflexive and spontaneous response is elicited. The response to the question about Mu indicates the practitioner's level of experiential realization of Mu. The teacher's query is called a "checking question," meant to plumb how deeply practitioners have plunged themselves into Mu, to determine whether they have broken through its opaqueness and have seen through this impenetrable barrier. In short, this practice of Mu is meant to open practitioners to a direct experience of seeing one's true nature and being awakened to one's true self.

I propose an approach to Jesus inspired by this Mu koan. In the practice with Mu, we sit in stillness, allowing our minds, hearts, and entire being to be immersed in Mu, setting aside all conceptual content and verbal formulation and simply being one with Mu. In the course of the practice, we begin to see, hear, touch, taste, smell, and envision everything from this perspective of being one with Mu.

In the Ignatian contemplative exercises recommended for the Second Week, as well as the Third and Fourth Weeks, I suggest an approach that brackets or sets aside the doctrinal and theological issues around the identity of Jesus and invite Christian and non-Christian seekers of the Way to open their minds, hearts, and entire being to simply immerse themselves in what is presented in the scriptural texts: to be one with Jesus. If we allow ourselves to see, hear, touch, taste, smell, and envision everything from the perspective of being one with Jesus, we may be opened to an encounter of the heart and enter into the heart and spirit of Jesus, therein being given a glimpse of the Way.

In short, the suggestion is to go forth into these contemplative exercises emptying out the conceptual content of what we understand by "Jesus," and only keeping in mind that we are fixing our gaze on Jesus as manifesting and embodying what we earnestly seek: the Way. I make this suggestion for

Christians who accept the doctrinal content of the Nicene Creed or other versions of it, as well as for people who do not do so but are open to an encounter with what remains unknown but may reveal the Way.

## The Holy Spirit

The term "Holy Spirit" does not appear as such in the main body of the text of the Spiritual Exercises.[11] In the set of guidelines that Ignatius provides for making decisions in life, called "Rules for Discernment of Spirits," he refers to the "good spirit," or that which illuminates, encourages, and strengthens us in making decisions in accordance with divine will. This good spirit is set in opposition to the "evil spirit," or the "enemy of our human nature," which disrupts, divides, and thwarts our attempts at living truthfully and integrally. Ignatius also refers to the good spirit in connection with "God and his angels."

In traditional Christian understanding, the Holy Spirit, the Third Person of the Holy Trinity, vivifies, sustains, and sanctifies the universe, bringing everything back to the divine fold. The work of the Holy Spirit undergirds the entire process of the Exercises, guiding and leading us through the stages of Purification, Illumination, and Union. The good spirit then, who guides us in making decisions for our own good and in accordance with divine will, ultimately refers back to this dynamic reality of the Holy Spirit in action in our day-to-day lives. Although not explicitly spelled out in Ignatius's text of the *SE*, the Third Person of the Trinity is also understood as right at the heart of what happens to the person undergoing the Exercises.

The word "spirit" comes from the Hebrew *ruah* (*pneuma* in Greek, *spiritus* in Latin), referring to the breath. My suggestion for this volume is to set aside the metaphysical notions associated with "spirit" and invite readers to relate this word to the palpable phenomenon of breathing that we do each moment of every day. In this way, readers coming from different religious backgrounds and faith commitments may find common ground in a shared and basic human experience—breathing—and therein may realize a deeper connection beyond religious and theological differences.

Readers familiar with Ignatian spirituality and the Exercises may raise an objection. Take away God, Jesus Christ, and the Holy Spirit from the Spiritual Exercises, and what remains? Such readers might question, was it not the mystical experience of the Triune God that Ignatius was graced with on the banks of the river Cardoner that formed the core of his spiritual life and vision?[12] How could we leave that out without compromising the integrity of Ignatius's message?[13] In doing so, don't we dilute or distort things beyond recognition, taking away the heart and soul of Ignatius's message?

In response, I ask for a deeper look at what has been outlined above, appealing for a second look to forestall possible misunderstanding or misinterpretation. Our intention here is not to remove these key terms from the Spiritual Exercises but rather to sidestep them and set aside their conceptual content, precisely to enable seekers to be more open to an encounter with the Mystery behind and beyond the words and names. This book is an invitation to sit in stillness and allow our hearts to open to a dimension that our human language can never adequately capture.

At this point, a Zen perspective can shed some light on the matter.

### Presenting Zen: A Frame of Reference

I have already compared some aspects of Zen with the Ignatian Exercises. Now I would like to describe key features of Zen to serve as a frame of reference for readers interested in but not too familiar with it, so that they can better understand what I mean by a "Zen perspective."

In brief, Zen is an invitation to a way of life that enables us to awaken to the dynamic reality of each present moment.[14] This way of life is centered on the practice of seated meditation (zazen) done on a regular basis, which paves the way for such awakening, bringing forth the three fruits of Zen: an integrated life characterized by concentration, the experience of seeing into one's true self or true nature, and the embodiment of awakening characterized by the cultivation of wisdom and compassion.[15]

Zazen entails a structure of components: taking a posture conducive to stillness, being aware of the breath, and silencing the mind to a point of stillness (discussed again in chapter 3). Zen (*Chan* in Chinese, *Son* in Korean) as handed down through centuries of tradition is known by four characteristics: (1) it does not rely on words or letters, (2) it is a special transmission outside of scriptural accounts, (3) it is transmitted from mind to mind from teacher to disciple, and (4) it leads to an experience of seeing one's true nature or true self, which is what "becoming a Buddha" (an awakened one) is all about.[16]

The first mark—that Zen does not rely on words or letters—means initially that we are not required to subscribe or adhere to a particular religious doctrine or viewpoint in order to practice Zen. Contrary to what some who study Zen in academic settings might say, Zen does not present itself as a philosophical doctrine or a religious teaching about reality. Rather, Zen offers a form of spiritual practice that is hands-on, practical, and down to earth, taking the Buddha's invitation as a cue: stop (the workings of your inquisitive mind) and see (what is, just as it is).

A reverse implication of this mark is that we are not

required to abandon or set aside our beliefs or religious standpoint in order to fully engage in Zen. Thus, Jews, Christians, Muslims, atheists, and other non-Buddhists, with their own particular religious and doctrinal views or lack of them, may practice Zen and continue to be Jews, Christians, Muslims, atheists, and so on as they continue in its sustained practice. The deepening of our practice may lead us to question certain assumptions or conceptual formulations of our beliefs, but such questioning can also lead to purification, clarification, and renewed understanding of our beliefs, rather than to their unreflective abandonment.[17]

Another, more important point conveyed by this first mark of Zen is that the Zen path opens us to a kind of experience that *as such* is beyond anything that words and conceptual formulations can articulate. The image of the proverbial finger pointing to the moon is usually brought in here, with words and concepts likened to the finger and the indescribable reality experienced in Zen likened to the moon shining in its lucid brilliance to anyone whose eyes are opened. Nevertheless, Zen tradition and practice have not stopped anyone from attempting to articulate what Zen is all about, as seen in the multitudes of volumes about it. The outcome is that attempts to render into words what is experienced in Zen come in different forms and may appear contradictory. What we see are fingers pointing in all directions, sometimes appearing to cancel one another out.

Given such a scenario, how are we to trust any verbal formulation about Zen, including this one? I would offer this response: "By their fruits you shall know them." That is, if whatever is said about that which cannot be said is wholesome and life-giving, leading to inner peace, humility, and compassion, then we can take such a statement as authentic, truly grounded, and worthy of trust.

The second mark of Zen is another way of saying the same

thing as the first: no scriptural text can do full justice to what Zen is all about. Yet Zen does not thereby reject scriptural texts but takes them to be like other verbal formulations, some more effective than others (in their role as "fingers").

Zen's third mark affirms the need to receive guidance from those who have themselves received guidance from teachers who in authentic ways have embodied the Zen life.[18]

The fourth mark of Zen emphasizes that the matter of Zen is about awakening to one's true self, seeing into one's true nature, and thereby arriving at genuine inner peace, giving way to humility, and opening to a life of compassion and service to others, following the example of the Buddha, the Awakened One.

Earnest practitioners of Zen are invited to take on a threefold set of attitudes, that of Great Trust, Great Doubt, and Great Resolve.[19]

Great Trust is based on the knowledge that we engage in this practice of Zen following in the footsteps and in the company of countless others, beginning with Shakyamuni Buddha himself. These practitioners have taken up Zen and come to an awakening, activating wisdom and compassion in their lives. This Great Trust is a deep-seated trust that goes even deeper as we continue in the practice, trusting that we in fact already are embodying that which we seek from the depths of our hearts: the awakening that opens us to a life of wisdom and compassion.

Great Doubt is the questioning that comes as we see the gap between what this practice is meant to bring about in our lives and the reality of how we continue to live our ordinary lives still mired in selfish ways and misled by delusional thoughts.

Great Resolve is precisely what comes about in realizing this gap, drawing forth all the spiritual energy we can muster in directing ourselves wholeheartedly to the practice. Every time we sit in meditation, we are drawn to sit fully engaged with our entire being, as a matter of life and death.

This earnestness in engaging in the practice is expressed in the verse recited as a closing chant each night during a Zen retreat, intoned by a designated cantor: "I humbly proclaim before the Sangha. Resolving the matter of birth and death is of prime importance. Everything goes quickly by like a fleeting arrow. Be mindful each moment. Do not let a moment pass by unaware!"

In sum, the Zen perspective that we refer to in examining the Ignatian Spiritual Exercises incorporates all the above features—the three components (posture, breathing, bringing the mind to stillness), the four marks (no reliance on words, special transmission outside of Scriptures, heart-to-heart or mind-to-mind transmission, and awakening and becoming a Buddha in seeing one's true self or true nature), and the three attitudes (trust, doubt, and resolve). As we proceed, we see how these play out and serve to highlight the key themes of the Exercises and cast them in a new light.

### Notes

[1]David Tracy, *Plurality and Ambiguity: Hermeneutics, Religion, Hope* (Chicago: University of Chicago Press, 1994), 12. Tracy's full citation reads as follows: "On historical grounds, classics are simply those texts that have helped found or form a particular culture. On more explicit hermeneutical grounds, classics are those texts that bear an excess and permanence of meaning, yet always resist definitive interpretation. In their production, there is always the following paradox: though highly particular in origin and expression, classics have the possibility of being universal in their effect." (Ibid., 12.)

[2]See David Lonsdale, *Eyes to See, Ears to Hear: An Introduction to Ignatian Spirituality* (Maryknoll, NY: Orbis Books, 2000), 13–33.

[3]Roger Haight, *Christian Spirituality for Seekers: Reflections on the Spiritual Exercises of Ignatius Loyola* (Maryknoll, NY: Orbis Books, 2012), xii.

[4]See Karen Armstrong, *A History of God* (New York: Vintage, 2004), and Jack Miles, *God: A Biography* (New York: Knopf, 1995).

[5]There is a long and solid Christian tradition of apophatic theology (the theological stance that God is ultimately beyond human understanding and articulation)—since Pseudo-Dionysius, and running through Thomas Aquinas, continuing within the Eastern Orthodox tradition and also in more recent theological formulations—also referred to as "negative theology," emphasizing the fundamental ineffability and unknowability of God. This notwithstanding, God-talk proliferates in a way that completely disregards this important stream of Christian thinking. In bringing a Zen perspective to bear on the Ignatian Exercises, a renewed appreciation of apophatic theology is in order.

[6]Gerald Benedict, *The God Debate: A New Look at History's Oldest Argument* (London: Watkins, 2013). For a clear and engaging account of the "revolution" in ways of talking about God, see Elizabeth A. Johnson, *Quest for the Living God: Mapping Frontiers in the Theology of God*, (New York: Bloomsbury, 2007).

[7]Norman Fischer, *Opening to You: Zen-Inspired Translations of the Psalms* (New York: Viking Compass, 2003), xxv.

[8]See Gregory A. Barker, *Jesus in the World's Faiths: Leading Thinkers from Five Religions Reflect on His Meaning* (Maryknoll, NY: Orbis Books, 2005).

[9]As the editor of an encyclopedia surveying the influence of Jesus in history put it, "to take a basic matter, nobody else in the world's history has the distinction of having that history divided for most human beings at his supposed point of entry into it." James Leslie Houlden, *Jesus in History, Thought and Culture: An Encyclopaedia* (2 volumes, Santa Barbara, CA: ABC-CLIO, 2003), p. xxv.

[10]See James Ishmael Ford and Melissa Myozen Blacker, *The Book of MU: Essential Writings on Zen's Most Important Kōan* (Boston: Wisdom Publications, 2011).

[11]The only place where Ignatius refers to the Spirit specifically is in the Appendix to the Exercises, in the section on "Rules for Thinking with the Church": "There is but one Spirit, which governs and directs us for the salvation of our souls, for the same Spirit and Lord, who gave us the Ten Commandments, guides and governs our Holy Mother Church" (Rule 13).

[12]Ignatius's own testimony of this mystical experience of the Trinity on the banks of the Cardoner can be found in *Autobiography of Ignatius of Loyola, with Related Documents*, ed. John C. Olin, trans. Joseph O'Callaghan (New York: Harper and Row, 1974), 39. This trinitarian motif, indeed central in Ignatius's spiritual vision, is a theme I hope to address in a future work of comparative theology, also in the light of Buddhist perspectives on ultimate reality. The work of John Keenan,

*The Meaning of Christ: A Mahayana Theology* (Maryknoll, NY: Orbis Books, 1989), addressing the christological question, is a pacesetter in this vein.

[13]Another feature of the Ignatian Exercises that those familiar with it from a Catholic perspective will note as missing from this treatment is his "Rules for Thinking with the Church." Given the intended readership of this work—taking Ignatius across traditional religious boundaries and seeking to retrieve his spiritual message for a wider community of spiritual seekers—I beg the reader's indulgence for now, as I hope to address this aspect of ecclesiology in global perspective in future writings.

[14]This is the working definition of Zen provided for those beginning the practice at our Maria Kannon Zen Center. See MKZC staff, ed., *Beginning Zen* (Dallas: MKZC Publications, 1999).

[15]See the section on "The Three Fruits of Zen" in the Introduction to this volume.

[16]For a more detailed exposition of the threefold structure and the four marks of Zen—as well as the three attitudes (addressed later)—see R. Habito, *Healing Breath: Zen for Christians and Buddhists in a Wounded World* (Boston: Wisdom Publications, 2006), chaps. 2, 3 and 4.

[17]On this point I am following the lead and the example of my own teacher in Zen, Yamada Kōun Rōshi, who welcomed Christians, Jews, and others as his Zen students. This approach is in direct contrast to his own teacher, Yasutani Hakuun Rōshi, who had emphasized that in order to do "authentic Zen," one needed to become a Buddhist and let go of any previous religious affiliation. For this, see Ruben Habito, "In Memoriam: Yamada Kōun, 1907–1989," *Buddhist Christian Studies* 10 (1990): 231-37.

[18]The vital importance of receiving guidance from an authorized Zen teacher is emphasized, so that the seeker may connect to the living community of practitioners—bearers of the tradition through centuries.

[19]These three attitudes are referred to as the "three essentials of Zen practice." See Philip Kapleau, ed., *Three Pillars of Zen*, rev. and exp. ed. (New York: Anchor Books, 1980), 64–66.

## 2

# Preliminary Guidelines for Entering the Path

In Ignatius's preliminary guidelines to his map for the inward journey, called the "Annotations," he defines "spiritual exercises" as

> every way of examining one's conscience, of meditating, contemplating, of praying vocally and mentally, and other spiritual activities as will be explained later. For just as strolling, walking and running are exercises for the body, so spiritual exercises is the name given to every way of preparing and making ourselves ready to get rid of all disordered affections so that, once rid of them, one might seek and find the divine will in regard to the disposition of one's life for the salvation of one's soul. (Ivens, 1.)

Here Ignatius simply assumes a view taken for granted in the context of his time, derived from its Greek heritage and carried on in Christian theological discourse. This view takes the term "spiritual" to refer to a realm distinct and separate from matters of the body and of the physical or material world. In this distinction, an underlying value judgment privileges the spiritual over the physical.

Ironically, a reverse valuation appears to prevail in our

contemporary world. We are immersed in a consumer-oriented and market-based global economy that feeds on ever-expanding human desires. The body beautiful is glorified. Images bombard us on all fronts, from full-page newspaper ads and fashion magazine covers to internet websites, with an underlying message tantamount to a cult of the body, telling us, "You *are* your body."

Zen teaching, in contrast, offers an integral vision of our human being, emphasizing the intrinsic unity of these two aspects of our existence. Such an integral vision sidesteps the dualistic view of spiritual-vs.-physical that Ignatius's definition implies. In this light we need to clarify our starting point for engaging in spiritual exercises and provide a working definition of the term that would be consonant with an integral vision of reality that overcomes the widely held dichotomous view.

In the common Preface found in all volumes of the series *World Spirituality: An Encyclopaedic History of the Religious Quest,* we find a working hypothesis offered by the editors that invites further conversation across different religious traditions: "The spiritual core is the deepest center of the person. It is here that the person is open to the transcendent dimension; it is here that the person experiences ultimate reality."[1]

Taking a cue and borrowing from the above, I use the following definition as the starting point for our map of the inward journey: *The term "spiritual exercises" denotes every way in which we connect with and come home to the innermost core of our being, whereby we are opened to the transcendent dimension and experience ultimate reality.* How then, in concrete terms, do we connect with or come home to the innermost core of our being?

In her autobiographical work *Long Quiet Highway,* Natalie Goldberg writes about an experience in ninth grade as her teacher Mr. Clemente switched off the lights and told everyone to just sit and listen to the rain outside. This was a pivotal moment in her life, coming at a time when she was struggling with issues of her identity and place in the big, wide world.

> And here was Mr. Clemente who asked me to listen to the rain, to connect a sense organ to something natural, neutral, good. He asked me to become alive. I was scared, and I loved it. . . . Thank God for that rain out of the window and for Mr. Clemente, who allowed us in the ninth grade to listen to it for no reason, in the middle of the day. That moment carried me a long way into my life.[2]

Goldberg's experience was occasioned by Mr. Clemente's instructions to stop what she and the other students in the class were doing and simply listen. This form of spiritual exercise—stopping whatever we may be doing and connecting a sense organ to something "natural, neutral, good"—is accessible and simple. In Goldberg's case it was the ear, to listen. Such an exercise could as easily apply to the other senses: seeing, smelling, tasting, and touching. This kind of spiritual exercise involves our whole being in the matter at hand—connecting through our senses, here and now, with the innermost core of our being.

Buddhist meditative practice that cuts across the various subtraditions and that is described in voluminous tomes throughout the centuries can be summed up in this short phrase: Stop and see.[3] Here, "seeing" refers not only to the sense of sight but to apprehending something, as when we say, "Oh, I see the point!" To be a Buddha—to be enlightened—is to see things as they really are. Meditative practice is a most effective way to move toward enlightenment.

One does not have to be a Buddhist or even profess some form of religious belief or affiliation to be able to stop and see, and thereby be touched and transformed at the innermost core of our being. This transformation can happen to any human being anytime, anywhere, with different levels of depth, intensity, and transformative power. It has happened to people throughout history, in all stages and walks of life, all over the world. The sages, mystics, and spiritual writers of the world's religious traditions witness to the fact that when humans somehow connect with the innermost core of their beings, something important and life-changing happens. For good or for ill, people to whom such a thing happens can never be the same.

In Natalie Goldberg's case, she identified that singular moment of stopping to listen to the rain in Mr. Clemente's class as the starting point of the many creative elements that sprang up in her own journey home to her true self. At the same time, however, she was not fully able to understand its significance: "I didn't know it then. At the time, I think, it made me too nervous—it was too naked, too uncontrolled, too honest."[4]

This point is the first stepping-stone in our attempt to retrieve the Spiritual Exercises from the religious and cultural background of medieval and early modern European Christendom, and to open it to our twenty-first-century globalized and multireligious society. We are reframing our understanding of "spiritual exercises" from a dichotomous view that separates the realm of the spirit from the realm of our bodily existence to a view that considers our human be-ing in all its dimensions as an integral whole. The spiritual is understood as dwelling at the core of our being, leading us to a realm beyond words—a realm of mystery.

To undertake spiritual exercises is to take up the invitation to stop and see for ourselves and to connect with this core. It is to traverse the path to which we are all called: the inward path toward home. Taking on a path of spiritual practice in a sustained and systematic way involves a resolution to turn our lives in this direction, beyond merely trying it out.

Of course, the path may also be for people who just want to check things out to see whether it works for them. But another time may come for such people, sooner or even much later, when they are ready to take on the path in a more engaged way.

We are ready when we come to a point in our lives where we ask earnestly, "What is the point of it all?" Then we are ready. We are truly seeking the one thing necessary in this life that we need to know or realize before we die, whenever that may be. We may come to this point at any stage of our lives—for example, when we are told we have a terminal illness. At such a time we experience a rude awakening, the realization that *I am going to die*. We might be confronting the pain of loss, loneliness, and our own mortality after a loved one dies. We may lose a long-held job, forcing us to take stock and ask, "What am I now to do with the rest of my life?" We may be shaken from the usual patterns of activity and living our humdrum lives in such a way that threatens or actually takes away things we had presumed were always going to be there for us. Something could come at us out of the blue, making us question, *Who am I? What have I been doing all this time? What is all this about?* On such occasions we find ourselves confronted with the big questions in a way we may never have experienced. *How can I live my life in a way that makes sense?*

In Ignatius's words, the Exercises are for those who have the earnest intent to "seek and find the Divine will in regard to the disposition of one's life for the salvation of one's soul" (Annotation I, Ivens, 1). In short, these matters are not just about rearranging the furniture in our lives so that we may go about things in a better way, live more spiritually, and so on. Rather, the issue is addressing head-on the big questions of our entire life and resolving to realign our lives according to what we envision as our ultimate destiny. As pointed out in the Zen chant toward the close of chapter 1, this is a matter of life and death. The Ignatian Spiritual Exercises are geared to enable us to cast aside whatever obstructs us from this one thing necessary in life and thereby be able to devote ourselves wholeheartedly to this pursuit.

*Who am I? What should I do with the rest of my life? How may I live my life so that I may be at peace with myself and be able to meet my death with no regret?* If we face these questions head-on, we are ready to accept the invitation to stop and see, launching into an inward journey toward self-discovery.

Zen is a centuries-old tradition whose key practice is summed up in these two words: *stop* and *see*. It has a long track record of enabling practitioners to see into their own true nature and live accordingly in its light. For those wrestling with the big questions in life, the Zen tradition offers this invitation and command: "Sit still!" Sitting in stillness with full attention in the here and now is a most direct way of coming home to the innermost core of one's being.

## Terms of Engagement for the Exercises

Ignatius's introductory notes contain recommendations for those about to embark on the inward journey. In Annotation 5 he emphasizes the importance of generosity and magnanimity of spirit, which entails openness and a willingness to take the appropriate steps to align oneself with the divine will toward the realization of one's ultimate destiny.

The normally prescribed way of undertaking the Exercises is to take time off from one's regular duties and normal schedule of activities; separate oneself from family, friends, and acquaintances; and stay in a retreat center or other dwelling conducive to peace and a degree of solitude. Ignatius outlines the benefits of this temporary separation and voluntary seclusion, pointing out in Annotation 20 that people are thus better able to devote themselves "all the more freely to the wholehearted search for what one's heart desires" (Ivens, 20).[5]

The "weeks" of the Spiritual Exercises do not necessarily entail seven days as such, but rather denote a suitable time frame for people engaging in the program to savor the fruit of each phase, shortened or extended as necessary. For people able to devote their full time and wholehearted effort to the Exercises in a place separate from their regular activities and in conditions conducive to stillness, the entire process normally takes about thirty days. For people not able to engage in the Exercises for the full thirty days, abbreviated forms—for periods of eight, five, or three days—are also offered.[6]

In Annotation 19 Ignatius makes provisions for those who, on account of public duties, family responsibilities, or other legitimate reasons, are unable to take time off to go to a separate place and devote their full time to undertaking the Spiritual Exercises. In such instances, the Exercises may be completed over an extended time covering from around eighteen to twenty-two months, during which the seeker takes sixty to ninety minutes each day to work with the Exercises and also visits weekly with a spiritual director to receive guidance on succeeding steps.

The chapters of this book follow the key movements of the Exercises that are situated within the four weeks, demarcating the stages of Purification, Illumination, and Union. In the course of describing these movements, I offer practical recommendations that readers can try out and apply in their own lives, in the mode of Annotation 19. People interested in following up are strongly urged to seek out an experienced spiritual director who can guide them through these movements to the intended outcome: awakening and personal transformation.

### The Spiritual Director and the Zen Teacher

Many people throughout the world—Jesuit and non-Jesuit, lay Christians or clergy, members of different religious communities—are certified to serve as spiritual directors for people undertaking the Ignatian Exercises. They are deemed qualified partly based on guidelines Ignatius laid down for such directors.

An important issue for spiritual directors is that they not hinder the process by explaining too much or giving their interpretations; instead, they should allow and enable seekers to experience the fruits of the Exercises directly for themselves. We keep this point of caution in mind throughout this book.

The role of a Zen teacher can be described in similar ways. Teaching something about Zen to others is not as important as walking with practitioners along the path of Zen and offering pointers for them to find the way on their own.[7]

We are invited to enter into an inward journey to a realm of the mystical, a realm of Mystery. These two terms, "mystical" and "mystery," derive from a Greek verb that means "to shut one's mouth (or eyes)." We are now dealing with an area that goes beyond words, or the ineffable. Yet, as embodied beings, we cannot escape the need to use words and concepts to convey what lies in the innermost depths of our hearts. We need to be constantly aware of this wondrous tension between words and that which the words seek to uncover.

The person who guides another on the inward journey

needs to be constantly aware of this tension and learn to be skillful in the use of words, concepts, doctrinal themes, and other forms of expression so that they serve to uncover, manifest, and reveal the Mystery rather than covering and hiding it from view. In fact, the true Spiritual Director—the One who can open our eyes, touch our hearts, and transform our being—is, after all, *not* the human being to whom this term refers. Rather, as we entrust ourselves to the Breath—to the Spirit—and are led deep into the stillness, if we keep our hearts open we will hear an inner voice that we recognize.

### Notes

[1] *World Spirituality: An Encyclopaedic History of the Religious Quest* (New York: Crossroads, 1997), xiv. Ewert Cousins wrote the common Preface for this series.

[2] Natalie Goldberg, *Long Quiet Highway: Waking Up in America* (New York: Bantam Books, 1993), 6, 5.

[3] In Sanskrit these terms correspond to *śamatha* and *vipaśyanā* (*vipassanā* in Pāli), technical terms in Buddhism that describe states of mind in the meditative state.

[4] Goldberg, *Long Quiet Highway*, 5.

[5] In the thirty-day retreat conducted for the Philippine seminarians who inspired the writing of this book, the twelve participants sat in stillness—Zen style, together in the same meditation hall, facing a wall—for eight to nine hours each day.

[6] In the life of a Jesuit, after one undertakes the full thirty-day period of the Spiritual Exercises soon after entrance into the Society of Jesus, one devotes an eight-day period annually for the Exercises. Three-day or five-day retreats are offered to people according to the time frame they are able to devote away from the normal course of their lives.

[7] See an account of the "Zen teacher as midwife," in R. Habito, *Healing Breath: Zen for Christians and Buddhists in a Wounded World* (Boston: Wisdom Publications, 2006), chap. 3.

# 3

# Who Am I? Why Am I Here?

## *The Principle and Foundation of the Spiritual Path*

At the Maria Kannon Zen Center in Dallas, during the orientation talks offered for people who come seeking guidance in beginning Zen practice, newcomers are asked, "Why Zen?" Responses to this question of what motivates people to begin Zen meditation generally fall into four categories.

1. People may be drawn to Zen out of curiosity. They may have read some books about Zen or heard some friends talk about it in fascinating ways, and they want to try it out for themselves.

2. People may want to practice Zen after having heard of the physical benefits that can result—reduced stress, lower blood pressure, and the ability to live at a slower pace and thus enjoy life more. According to some reports, Zen practice can even help cure cancer and other physical ailments. If Zen improves health, that's a good motivator.

3. Some people want to try Zen in order to deepen their spiritual lives. They may be seeking inner peace in the midst of personal struggles. They may feel a need for centering themselves in the midst of a hectic and busy life with many external demands and responsibilities. The practice of Zen,

which involves stopping all we are doing and paying attention in silence, directly addresses these kinds of inner needs. If we turn to this practice of sitting in stillness and continue it in a regular and sustained way, in due time the various aspirations we had as we began generally come to bear fruit in our lives.

4. People considering the big questions of human existence—"Who am I?" "What is the point of all this?" "What are the meaning and purpose of my life?" "Faced with the fact that I will someday die, how can I live my life fully, with a true understanding and appreciation of what it's all about?"—turn to Zen in the hope that the practice of meditation may open the way to resolving these questions.

Beginners usually receive introductory instructions through orientation talks at a Zen center, and after a period of trying out the practice of seated meditation, they are ready to meet the teacher. In the first formal meeting between practitioner and teacher, the teacher asks that question: "Why Zen?" or "Why do you want to begin Zen practice?" Then the teacher gives the student formal instructions for proceeding. This direction may be as simple as an encouragement to continue sitting—focusing the mind on the breath and counting up to 10 with each out-breath, and then going back to 1. After practitioners have become accustomed to this practice, they may set aside the counting and just let the mind follow the breath with each inhaling and exhaling movement. Once mastering that practice, they are ready to launch into the deepest form of Zen practice: "just sitting" (*shikan taza* in Japanese)—a way of sitting still and paying attention to each moment in the here and now, without judging, evaluating, or anticipating anything, and simply letting the mind enter into stillness.

On the surface, "just sitting" sounds simple enough, but anyone who has ventured into this practice even for a short while can readily acknowledge how difficult it is. The mind can be so unwieldy, restless, and fidgety, going all over the place except the one place where it is called to be: the here and now. Even so, as one continues this practice in a sustained way—not over weeks or months but perhaps after years and years—somehow moments come when one is simply *there, just sitting.* In such moments, time stops, and it is just *now*; all space converges, and it is just *here*.

Such a moment may also come when one is not necessarily in a formal mode of seated meditation but while leisurely taking a walk, sipping coffee, lounging on a sofa doing nothing in particular, and so on. The phrase that emerges in seeking to describe such moments is "just this," in the concrete particularity of the scenario where it happens. It may be triggered by a sound, like the barking of a dog, the chirping of a bird, or a sneeze of a person nearby. It may be triggered by a visual scene, like a tree, a rock, a cloud, or a wall. The moment may also be triggered by a sensation—a gentle breeze caressing one's skin or the sudden pain as one unwittingly steps on something sharp. Whatever the concrete circumstances, at this moment the whole universe collapses into *just this.* Just sitting is a most direct way of opening oneself to such moments.

What I am referring to in using the expression "just this" is not to be construed as implying a "this" as opposed to "that over there." *Just this* swallows up everything else—all time and all space—such that there is nothing but *just this.*

In such moments the questions of "Who am I?" "Why am I here?" and "What are the meaning and purpose of my life?" recede from the horizon, as if they have been answered by no longer needing to be asked. In other words, these questions are resolved in being dissolved into the experience of *just this.* Who? Why? Wherefore? *Just this.* There is no longer a need to ask. One's life is whole, complete, and at peace, and one is able to live from day to day with equanimity, joy, and a heart full of compassion for all beings. (We come back to this later.)

Individuals grappling with the big questions in Zen practice may also be given what we may call an entry-level koan by their teacher, as a way of resolving those questions that propel each of them to the practice. Many compilations of koans are readily available in English translation.[1] The koans "What is the sound of one hand?"[2] and "Who hears?" are two examples of entry-level koans, as is the koan Mu, which we considered briefly in chapter 1: "A monk asked [Zen master] Jōshū in all earnestness, 'Does a dog have Buddha nature or not?' Jōshū answered, 'Mu!'"

People given this koan are advised to forget about the monk, Jōshū, the idea of "Buddha nature," and the concepts associated with it, and to simply accept this daunting and incomprehensible syllable "Mu" as the guide to opening a realm that presents a mystery to the beginner. It is like being ushered by the hand into a place of complete darkness, and our only light is this very concrete and dynamic activity going on within ourselves—that is, the breath.

But we are immediately faced with a stumbling block. How are we to take this invitation to set aside all doctrines and concepts, and place a meaningless and opaque syllable such as "Mu" at the center of our spiritual practice? We are told time and again that "Mu" is not even a word in the ordinary sense, that is, an utterance with a referent or meaning. Instead, "Mu" is a plain sound or syllable that we are to keep repeating with the out-breath. In fact, many people give up on Mu because they cannot get past this initial problem.

To move beyond this initial barrier requires a great degree of trust in the Zen tradition, in the whole lineage of ancestors and adepts who have taken up this practice and found in it the wellsprings of transformative power for their own lives, as well as in the teacher who is guiding us in this practice. To people who tell me that they are ready to give up on this practice, I say, "Hang in there! Rely on the Great Trust that you are being led deeper into a Mystery that is your true self. Trust that you are in good hands. Let go. Hang on to the breath. Plunge more deeply into the stillness, into Mu!"

With what may seem to be a near-blind trust as our sole beacon, we are instructed to be attentive in each moment with Mu as the point of focus—to breathe out with our mind focused on the silent sound of "Muuu," breathing in and repeating this again and again with every out-breath. In so doing, our entire being is brought into focus in the here and now. We become totally engrossed, absorbed, and dissolved in Mu. This practice enables us to develop a state of mind that is fully here in each moment in a naked state of awareness, a state of being that is called samādhi, a kind of undifferentiated consciousness wherein we are rapt in inner peace and equilibrium.

Recall that this koan is offered to those of us who come to Zen practice with a burning question in life, centered on "Who am I?" The practice of sitting in silence and enabling our entire being to come to full focus in Mu is a way of bringing us into the depths of our very being, beyond words and concepts, leading us to a direct experience that opens up the answer to this burning question.

We who take to Zen practice with this Great Trust that we are in good hands, even though we are totally in the dark as to what it is all about, also grapple with Great Doubt, as we have already noted. We may ask ourselves, *If this is the way to the realization of my true self, how come I don't seem to be getting anywhere? Maybe I'm just not one of those meant to "get it" in the first place, so why should I continue in this arduous practice?* And that Great Doubt can give rise to Great Resolve: *If my entire life banks on this, then I will give it all I have and not relent until I get to the bottom of it.*

Though some of us may be graced with something like beginner's luck, or auspicious karma that becomes like a backwind that propels us to go readily and deeply into the practice, for most people it takes time—not months but years of practice. But for those who persevere in the practice in a sustained way, at some point—whether through a gradual process of sweeping away the layers that cloud the mind little by little and receiving momentary glimpses of the sun along the way, or in an unexpected thunderous instant where everything that had blocked their view is all of a sudden blown away—they see the light as clear as the noonday sun, and the indubitable answer emerges to the "Who am I?" question.

Practitioners who arrive at this experience are opened to a new horizon, an entirely new way of looking at themselves and at the entire universe. At the same time, they realize that nothing has changed; in the words of a Zen chant, "Mountains are high, valleys are low, water is wet, the eyes are horizontal, the nose is vertical." Everything is just as it is. It's *just this*! Yet it is nothing at all like we had imagined *this* to be.

This breakthrough experience in Zen—called "kenshō" [seeing into one's own true nature]—is an experience of directly knowing who *I am* and also seeing everything in the entire universe in this light, *just as it is*. The experience ushers in deep peace, joy, and gratitude.

This is the great matter at hand: the Principle and Foundation, in Ignatian words, of Zen practice. This is the point of it all, illuminating the answer to the questions of "Who am I?" and "Why I am here?" In short, what we see in this breakthrough experience already contains in itself all that we need and could ever want for our lives. From this point on, we are called simply to live out this Principle and Foundation, unpacking it as it were—tasting it; realizing and appreciating it more and more deeply; embodying it in every thought, word, and deed from day to day and moment to moment for the rest of our lives and beyond. This call is to live experiencing every moment as *just this*, in a way that breaks away from the humdrum of linear time and opens to a glimpse of the eternal.

Zen practice is not to be conceived in terms of a linear progression with a starting point, middle course, and finish line. A more apt way of depicting it would be in terms of a spiral movement that moves ever closer to its center, to which every step is directed and out of which every step proceeds.

This Principle and Foundation of Zen, this transformative experience of seeing into one's true nature, is thus both the starting point and the ending point, the Alpha and the Omega of Zen practice. To realize truly and fully embody this Principle and Foundation of Zen is the endeavor of a lifetime. The experience cannot be readily expressed in verbal terms, like a pat answer that serves as a magic solution that will resolve all of our problems and answer all of our questions. The ineffable character of this matter at hand is precisely to what the Zen dictum of "not relying on words or letters" refers.

This dictum serves as a disclaimer that such verbal or conceptual expressions will not help take us where Zen practice is leading us. Zen invites us to taste it ourselves, to see it with our own eyes in the midst of the stillness, in actual engagement in seated meditation. Given this emphasis on tasting and realizing for ourselves, I invite readers who feel drawn to it to visit a nearby Zen community with an authorized teacher and to start the practice for themselves.

The underlying motivation that propels many of those who take on Zen practice on the one hand and those who engage in the Spiritual Exercises on the other appear to coincide. The motivator is no less than the burning desire to resolve the ultimate questions of life for ourselves: "Who am I?" "Why am I here?" and "What are the meaning and purpose of my life?" However, on the surface at least, the responses that these two paths of spirituality offer could not be more different.

Zen offers no systematic verbal formulation of the answers to the meaning of it all. It simply invites us to plunge right into the practice of seated meditation, with a posture conducive to silence, paying attention to one's breath, and allowing the mind to be still in the here and now. This invitation is to taste and see for ourselves.

## The Ignatian Principle and Foundation

In contrast to the Zen way of unknowing that marks the formal entry into the path, Ignatius offers a summary statement right at the beginning of the Spiritual Exercises that spiritual seekers are advised to accept and take to heart in launching the inward journey. To seekers who ask, "What are the meaning and purpose of my life?" Ignatius has an unequivocal response. He says, "This is what it's all about, and this is why you are undertaking these Exercises, so trust me and take it from here." He does not offer any particular meditative or contemplative exercises for seekers to absorb or to delve into it experientially, but simply makes a didactic statement: "This is it. Take it from here."

He presents what he calls the Principle and Foundation (*Principio y Fundamento*) at the opening section of his written text of the *Spiritual Exercises*, laying out who we are and why we are here in plain terms, derived from his own Roman Catholic understanding and worldview. In doing so, he also clarifies why anyone would undertake these Exercises in the first place: to live our lives more fully in accordance with, and not contrary to, the very purpose of why we are here on earth:

> We human beings are created to praise, reverence, and serve God our Lord, and in doing so, attain our eternal salvation. All other things on the face of the earth are created for human beings, so that they may help us in fulfilling the purpose for which we are created. From this it follows that we are to use them as much as they help us in attaining our purpose, and ought to rid ourselves of them so far as they hinder us in this. For this it is necessary to make ourselves indifferent to all created things in all that is allowed to the choice of our free will and is not prohibited; so that, on our part, we want not health rather than sickness, riches rather than poverty, honor rather than dishonor, long rather than short life, and so in all the rest, desiring and choosing only what is most conducive for us to the purpose for which we are created.[3]

Right at the beginning, Ignatius thus throws something like a koan to those who would venture on this inward path with him as guide. To people who have come to a point of asking the big questions of life in earnest, and who are ready to receive his guidance in confidence and trust, Ignatius hurls these words, in effect: "You are here on earth to live in praise, reverence, and service of the One who is the Infinite Source and Ultimate Goal of your very being. This is the way for you to realize Eternal Life."

Regarding Ignatius's proposition that our very meaning and purpose of being on this earth are to "praise, reverence, and serve God our Creator and Lord," I suggest that we set aside our previously held images and concepts of God, as suggested in chapter 1. Instead of imagining a white-robed, bearded, and kindly old man up in the sky—thought of as almighty and all-knowing, whom we are to "praise, reverence, and serve"—let us look to the horizon that is "so close we can't see it, yet so far away that we cannot reach it," as the poet Norman Fischer describes. Be still and listen from the depths of our own hearts.

Let us now examine individually the four points of Ignatius's statement of the Principle and Foundation.

1. *We are created "to praise, reverence, and serve God our Lord, and in doing so, attain our eternal salvation."* Ignatian language seems to indicate a means-end relationship between the two clauses. That is, it seems to mean that we "praise, reverence, and serve God our Creator and Lord" (here on earth) in order to "attain our eternal salvation" (in the next life). This reading holds us in a dualistic frame of mind, taking our life here on earth as a kind of "testing ground" as to whether we will merit eternal salvation in the next life, based on whether we do what we are supposed to do—that is, "praise, reverence, and serve." This reading may go unquestioned in the minds of many who undertake the Ignatian Exercises coming from a certain Christian theological mind-set.

However, I suggest that we may also take it in the following way: "to praise, reverence, and serve God our Creator and Lord" is in its essence to embody what the phrase "attain our eternal salvation" is all about. In other words, attaining our eternal salvation is made manifest through our every thought, word, and action, as "praise, reverence, and service toward God our Creator and Lord." Thus, we are able to let go of the means-end, earth-heaven dualism and be opened to an experience of encounter with Mystery right in the midst of our lives, seen in the light of that someone so intimate and yet so beyond reach on the horizon of our mind.

What does it mean to praise God? Again, Norman Fischer's description of the audience for his poetry speaks to us here: "someone much more silent and much more profoundly receptive than any human being could possibly be," and yet also (someone) "both so close to me I can't see it and so far away I can never reach it." Without needing to conjure any image in our minds, we keep that silent, intimate, and yet unreachable someone on the horizon as we consider what it means to "praise." Since that "silent, intimate, yet unreachable someone" is not an object in the proper sense of the word, it cannot be the object of my or anybody else's praise.

Yet we are enjoined to praise God. So, if "to praise"—distinguished from saying empty words of flattery—means to acknowledge in thought, word, and deed whatever is praiseworthy, then living uprightly and true to ourselves in a way that is accountable to that silent someone who is intimately within us as well as way beyond us is a most fitting way of giving praise, not just in words, but in and through our entire way of life.

A well-known saying of second-century theologian Irenaeus of Lyons comes to the fore in this regard: "The human being fully alive is the glory of God" [*Gloria Dei vivens homo*]. Living the fullness of our humanity—getting up in the morning, eating breakfast, going to work, eating lunch, relaxing with friends, going back home to the family, doing our mundane tasks—is giving glory and praise to God.

We might come up with a Zen koan on this: How do we "praise God" while washing dishes? If we venture an answer by showing the motions of washing dishes over a sink and then lifting up our head to heaven and saying, "Praise be to God," we fail the koan. Instead, consider that the very act of washing the dishes with dutiful and yet relaxed attention is the acceptable answer to this koan. The same holds true for everything else in our daily lives. We get up in the morning, we eat breakfast, we go to work, we take a walk—each and every thing becomes all praise and glory, fully manifest.

What does it mean to "reverence" or "revere" God? It is to acknowledge in thought, word, and action whatever we encounter in our daily lives as holy: to gaze at a sunset or at a starlit night, to watch a newborn baby asleep in his mother's arms, to water the plants, to avoid stepping on a bug on the sidewalk, to make the effort to live more simply, or to recycle waste products and avoid squandering resources as a way to stem the ecological destruction of the earth.

What does it mean to "serve" God? Maintaining that "silent, intimate, yet unreachable someone," neither object nor subject, as our horizon of awareness serves God. "Serving" means seeing to it that needs are met—by helping a friend or stranger, visiting a sick person or doing a random act of kindness, sweeping the floor and washing the dishes, doing what needs to be done. It is living from day to day no longer seeking our own self-interest but offering our entire being so that we can contribute in our own little ways to accomplishing what needs to be done in this broken world.

And here is the good news. Each thought, word, and action of ours—as well as mountains and rivers, the sun, the moon, the great wide earth, birds and fish, earthworms and caterpillars, and everything that exists as such . . . all lifted up in praise, reverence, or service—becomes a gateway to that unknown. A door opens to a glimpse of the eternal, right there manifested in and through these thoughts, words, or acts—all things in the universe seen in their concrete particularity. These are moments when we experience, in a direct bodily way, right here and now, the why and wherefore of our very human existence, the Principle and Foundation of the spiritual life.

In these moments we are able to exclaim, as Peter did at

the scene of the transfiguration, "It is good to be here!" In such moments we can say, "For this I was born, and now I can die in peace." Looking back as we lie on our deathbed and see the panoramic vista of our entire life, these moments stand out and bring home to us the realization that it is all worth it. We are in the midst of it all the time, but in these concrete moments in this journey of life we are brought to a direct awareness that we have touched the eternal and the eternal has touched us.

2. *"All other things on the face of the earth are created for human beings, so that they may help us in fulfilling the purpose for which we are created."* Here Ignatius is echoing a theological view based on the book of Genesis (1:28), which depicts human beings as "the summit of creation," assigned to have dominion over all other creatures and for whose service all other creatures were created. Today, with our knowledge of and concern for ecology, we are all too aware of the destructive effects that human hubris has wrought upon our earth community as a whole, fanned by this biblically supported theological view of humans being the summit of creation. Many Christian theologians have pointed out the problematic character of this view, calling for a reexamination of this concept, proposing ways of rereading those passages in Genesis, and emphasizing "stewardship" rather than "dominion."[4]

Noted thinkers have come to emphasize that our ongoing ecological crisis is more than a problem of technology. It is fundamentally a religious and theological problem that needs to be addressed at that level. In the wake of the heightened ecological consciousness of our age, we can take Ignatius to task, with all due respect, and seek a different way of articulating how we human beings relate to all other beings on earth.

Without going into a detailed explanation, we might

revise Ignatius's second point to read, "All other things on the face of the earth are created also to praise, reverence, and serve God our Creator and Lord, so that together with human beings they may help in fulfilling the purpose for which we are all created."

As such, we human beings can see ourselves not as having "dominion over" but rather as existing in community with all other things on earth, living and nonliving, as St. Francis of Assisi, several centuries before Ignatius, realized and proclaimed in his own life. Thus, we may "praise, reverence, and serve God our Creator and Lord" with Brother Sun, Sister Moon, Brother Elephant, Sister Ladybug, Brother Tree, Sister Flower, and so on. In short, each and every element in this universe of ours—mountains and rivers, grasses and trees, pebbles and sand, dogs and cats and earthworms and butterflies—each in its own way, just by being what it is, already fulfills "the why and wherefore of their existence." In simply being as they are, they unabashedly "praise, reverence, and serve God our Creator and Lord" in their own unique and glorious ways.

3. *"We are to use them as much as they help us in attaining our purpose, and ought to rid ourselves of them so far as they hinder us in this."* Given the modern consciousness, Ignatius's third point seems problematic. But we can see this point as addressing our ability to make choices in our life on earth.

4. *"It is necessary to make ourselves indifferent to all created things in all that is allowed to the choice of our free will and is not prohibited; so that, on our part, we want not health rather than sickness, riches rather than poverty, honor rather than dishonor, long rather than short life, and so in all the rest, desiring and choosing only what is most conducive for us to the purpose for which we are created."* As with his third point, Ignatius's fourth statement speaks to our ability to make proper choices.

Our own destiny and that of everyone around us depends on how we exercise our choices, whether they are done in accordance with the why and wherefore of our human existence. In other words, all the choices we make in life, from the small ones to the big ones, are to be set in terms of whether they enable us to "praise, reverence, and serve God our Creator and Lord." The "indifference" that Ignatius speaks about, which has become a key notion in Jesuit spirituality, is not to be mistaken for an uncommitted or emotionally detached stance but is instead a stance that comes out of the inner freedom of an individual totally dedicated to a life of praise, reverence, and service. We look at this task later in chapter 7, "The Quality of Freedom," when we consider Ignatian guidelines for making choices in life.

## What's Love Got to Do with It?

In setting forth the Principle and Foundation of the spiritual life at the beginning of the Exercises, Ignatius uses the term "praise, reverence, and service," yet does not bring in the word "love." Toward the end of this volume, we look back at the Principle and Foundation from the perspective of the summit of the Exercises—the Contemplation on Divine Love. At that point of our sojourn through the Ignatian Exercises we will be able to appreciate how Love underlies these three attitudes and empowers and enlightens every thought, word, and action—every choice we are called to make in this life.

In this connection, David Fleming, SJ, offers the following adaptation of the Ignatian Principle and Foundation:

The goal of our life is to live with God forever. God, who loves us, gave us life. Our own response of love allows God's life to flow into us without limit. All the things in this world are gifts of God, presented to us so that we can know God more easily and make a return of love more readily. As a result, we appreciate and use all these gifts of God insofar as they help us develop as loving persons. But if any of these gifts become the center of our lives, they displace God and so hinder our growth toward our goal. In everyday life, then, we must hold ourselves in balance before all of these created gifts insofar as we have a choice and are not bound by some obligation. We should not fix our desires on health or sickness, wealth or poverty, success or failure, a long life or short one. For everything has the potential of calling forth in us a deeper response to our life in God.[5]

Here Fleming makes explicit what Ignatius has not yet brought into the forefront for spiritual seekers just about to begin the Exercises. The inward journey we are about to be ushered into finds its culmination in an experience of Divine Love, an experience that inevitably transforms our lives, so that we may be able to live the rest of our lives no longer in pursuit of self-seeking ambition but as a gift offered back in love for the Love so profusely and unconditionally received.

The Principle and Foundation is presented at the entrance to the inward journey that is the Ignatian Exercises, as a response to the spiritual seeker asking the big questions of human existence: "Who am I?" "Why am I here?" and "What are the meaning and purpose of my life?" Summing up our reflections so far, I offer the following as an adaptation of the spirit of the Principle and Foundation.

Consider the Zen master who offers the inscrutable Mu koan to a beginning practitioner who is asking the big questions. That master is implicitly saying, "You may not understand this yet, but take this in trust, and you will see." In the same way, the spiritual seeker knocking on Ignatius's door is told,

> Take this in trust. You may not understand this yet, but there is an unknown someone who is closer to you than you can imagine, while remaining beyond your reach—someone who cares for you, who wants to see the best in you. You are accountable to that someone, who will also empower you and inspire you to live your best life, cherishing all that is praiseworthy and holy, offering yourself in service of others, choosing only what your heart tells you is best for you and for everyone else. As you live in this way, it will be given to you beyond any doubt. *That* is why you are here on earth. *That* is your gateway to eternal life.

The next questions are, "How can we live in that way?" and "Where do we go from here?" The Zen master says, "Just sit and be still." Or to those practicing with the Mu koan, "Pour your whole mind and body and whole being into Mu with each out-breath." In contrast, Ignatius invites us into the First Week of the Exercises with more detailed instructions.

### Notes

[1]See Yamada Kōun, *The Gateless Gate* (Boston: Wisdom Publications, 2004), for a well-known koan collection, with a Zen master's lucid commentaries on each of the cases.

[2]Mistakenly cited in popular usage as "What is the sound of one hand clapping?"

[3]My adapted English translation is based on consulting the Mottola and Mullan translations, revised for inclusive language. See Anthony Mottola, *The Spiritual Exercises of St. Ignatius* (New York: Image

Books, 1964), and Elder Mullan, SJ, *The Spiritual Exercises of St. Ignatius of Loyola, Translated from the Autograph* (New York: P. J. Kenedy and Sons, 1914).

[4]John B. Cobb Jr., Jurgen Moltmann, Leonardo Boff, Rosemary Radford Reuther, Catherine Keller, Sallie McFague, and increasing numbers of others have published works in the relatively new field of ecotheology.

[5]In David L. Fleming, SJ, *The Spiritual Exercises of St. Ignatius: A Literal Translation and a Contemporary Reading* (St. Louis: Institute of Jesuit Sources, 1978), 22 (slightly revised for inclusive language).

# PART TWO

# PURIFICATION

*A spiritual awakening can be occasioned by the realiza-
tion, "My life is a mess." It may be a nagging feeling over a
period of time, tugging at me and telling me in various kinds
of ways how I am not living my life quite as I would like to
live it. I may sometimes wake up in the middle of the night
and in a moment of lucidity, tinged with a pang of regret felt
from the pit of my stomach, see how I am wasting my life
with trivialities. Underlying all this is a deep longing to get
out of this mess, which is perhaps due in part to unfortunate
circumstances beyond my control, a string of bad decisions
I may have made, or intermeshing combinations of these.*

*In Zen Buddhism the point of launching on the path of
Transformation is called "awakening the Bodhi mind." It is
marked by a sense of freshness, eagerness, and resolve, much
like that of the monk who one day asked Zen Master Jōshū
in all earnestness, "I have just entered the monastery. I beg
you, Master, please give me instructions."*

*The master replied, "Have you eaten your rice gruel?"*

*The monk answered, "Yes."*

*At this, Jōshū said, "Then go wash your bowls."*

*That resolve is the determination that one cannot and will*

51

not rest until one gets to the bottom of it all and finds that which will give one true inner peace. Augustine referred to this notion when he wrote, "Our hearts are restless until they rest in Thee" (Confessions I, 1-2). In the case of Ignatius, he felt new stirrings during his period of recuperation as he noticed the different interior movements within him, now making him feel disgust for his former life and buoying him up at the prospect of a new life in God's service. Noticing these different interior movements launched Ignatius into this path of Transformation. Taking stock of his life, he realized, putting it in contemporary terms, that there was much work to be done.

This work to be done belongs to the stage of Purification. The next four chapters address themes that mark key movements in this stage: preliminary guidelines (in Ignatian terms, the Annotations), clarifying and articulating the goal (Principle and Foundation), realizing our human condition as in need of healing (First Week, part one), and moving in the direction toward recovery (First Week, part two).

One who launches on the path of Zen first undergoes preliminary orientation—including instructions on how to sit and how to maintain mindfulness in daily life—and then is given the task at hand in a one-to-one encounter with the teacher. In the background is the understanding that one is engaging in this practice to resolve the fundamental question of our human condition, referred to in Buddhism as dukkha (dissatisfaction, dis-ease, existential suffering). The path of overcoming dukkha is launched as one comes to understand and seeks to address its root causes, identified as the three poisons of greed, ill will, and ignorance, as manifested in our individual lives as well as on the corporate level in our ailing contemporary global society.

4

# The Human Condition

## *In Need of Healing*

As Zen practitioners gather together to sit in community, selected verses from Buddhist scriptural texts are normally chanted in unison after the period of formal sitting. The following chant, called "Verse of Purification," usually heads the list:

> *All harmful karma ever committed by me since*
> *of old*
> *On account of my beginningless greed, anger,*
> *and ignorance*
> *Born of my body, mouth, and consciousness*
> *Now I atone it all.*

Practitioners recite or chant this aloud in unison with all the others, with palms joined facing everyone, or in some cases facing the altar—usually with a Buddhist icon, which could be a figure of Kannon or Kuan-yin, the Shakyamuni Buddha, Maitreya Buddha, or one of the great Bodhisattvas. In the chant, one acknowledges one's own part in causing all the suffering, pain, evil, violence, and other harmful and undesirable things that have happened and continue to happen in this world of ours as "born of my body, mouth, and consciousness"—in short, as coming from my actions, words, thoughts, and attitudes. This confession is a heartfelt statement of one's complicity in all the harm that has ever been done to anybody on earth since the world began.

In the concluding line, "Now I atone it all," the word "atone" is based on a Chinese/Japanese compound that includes in its broad meaning "acknowledge," "confess," "repent," "make reparation," "cleanse," and "purify." The fortuitous word "atone" in the English translation here, which I first heard in this context at the Zen Mountain Monastery in Mount Tremper, New York, under the guidance of the late abbot John Daido Loori, and which I have also adapted for use at our own Maria Kannon Zen community, allows us to draw out another profound dimension as part of the chant's intent. We can take "atone" in hyphenated form, "at-one," whereby the verse is understood to mean that, in so chanting from the heart, I make myself "at one" with all the "harmful karma ever committed by me since of old"; by that very fact I acknowledge my responsibility for the harms and profess my willingness to bear whatever karmic consequences they may generate or have generated in the world, in my own body, mouth, and consciousness.

This theme does not seem to be addressed in great detail in many of the books on Zen intended for a general audience, but an awareness of evil, suffering, and our shared complicity is an underlying theme in the Zen path. The important aspect inseparably connected with this point is the transformative and healing power that Zen practice can bring to this world marked by so much suffering as a result of the harmful karma that each and every one of us commit. This theme, however, resonates deeply with the path that Ignatius has forged for the seeker following him in the Spiritual Exercises, as he lays out the task of the First Week.

The First Week provides an opportunity for us to take a straight look at and reflect on the problematic state of our human condition, spelling out the features of that harmful karma in great detail. The meditations here are meant to confront us with the stark realities of human sin, guilt, evil, and death in a way that is up close and personal.[1] We are then invited to move on to a radically new way of life, freed from the bondage of sin through *metanoia*, a total transformation of mind and heart.

Recognizing and admitting that all is not well can be a pivotal moment in our journey through life, a launching pad for embarking on a spiritual path. In twelve-step programs, which have proven to be rather effective in helping people overcome personal addictions and disorders of different kinds, admitting that a problem exists is a requisite starting point toward recovery.

We live in a milieu where the notion of sin has been pushed under the rug of our cultural consciousness. The Exercises thus call our attention to a dimension that many of our contemporaries tend to overlook or set aside rather than confront and address. We might take a hint from the fact that the word "sin" in English is *die Sünde* in German, related to "asunder," "separated," or "broken apart." This notion is what comes to the fore of our consciousness as we examine the situation of our world today: our global community is separated, ruptured, wounded, broken.

### State of the World, Sin of the World

Here are some facts that bring us face to face with our ailing global community:

- Twenty-one thousand children under the age of five die of malnutrition and related causes every day.

- Almost 2 billion people in the world live in conditions of "multidimensional poverty" (based on a set of measurable factors), including acute deprivation not just in food but also in health, education, and standard of living.
- More than 1 billion people in the world live without access to safe water, and 2.6 billion live without proper sanitation.
- Three hundred fifty-eight of the world's billionaires' combined income exceeds the amount of the combined annual incomes of countries with 45 percent of the world's population.
- In 2010, 43.7 million people were forcibly displaced from their homes, the highest number in fifteen years.
- Species are going extinct at more than one thousand times the natural rate, escalating the loss of the biodiversity of our planet.[2]

These statistics reflect a global human family in a broken, severely dysfunctional state. Although we human beings may pride ourselves on being "rational animals," what we see happening in our global society is far from rational. There are state-sponsored and other forms of organized (or unorganized) military violence perpetrated by groups of human beings against other groups in declared and undeclared wars in different parts of the world. We are bombarded by reports of violent acts that incite terror, planned and executed for political aims. Besides the kinds of violence using weaponry, violence is perpetrated against millions of women ensnared in pernicious sex trafficking rings in many parts of the world. Violence takes place against children and minors by people who use them as objects of sexual gratification. There is also the violence of the structural or systemic kind, brought about by a global economic system that deprives significant segments of our world population of the basic necessities or of the right to life itself.

In an encyclical titled *Sollicitudo Rei Socialis* (1987), Pope John Paul II named as "structural sin" the situation of our global society with its unjust structures that consign hundreds of millions of our fellow human beings to dehumanizing poverty while a very small and privileged segment of the population wallows in excessive wealth, conspicuous consumption, and unmitigated luxury: "'Sin' and 'structures of sin' are categories which are seldom applied to the situation of the contemporary world. However, one cannot easily gain a profound understanding of the reality that confronts us unless we give a name to the root of the evils which afflict us."[3]

In the same document, in analyzing and presenting various features of the notion of structural sin that characterizes our global predicament, John Paul II offers a hint as to tracing its causes and thereby addressing it at its root:

I have wished to introduce this type of analysis above all in order to point out the true nature of the evil which faces us with respect to the development of peoples: it is a question of a moral evil, the fruit of many sins which lead to "structures of sin." To diagnose the evil in this way is to identify precisely, on the level of human conduct, the path to be followed in order to overcome it.[4]

In short, the brokenness of our global family, while analyzable in terms of economic, political, cultural, historical, and other factors, is essentially a question of "moral evil, the fruit of many sins." This way of putting it calls attention to those human attitudes as well as "levels of human conduct" that lie behind and generate these structures of sin, including the way we live our lives, the way we relate to one another as individual human beings, and the way we humans relate to the earth and the natural world that is the matrix of our life. All these issues together constitute the sin of the world.

## In Need of Healing in Our Personal Lives

As I go through my life, I may notice—through self-reflection, certain unexpected moments of lucid insight, or a process of therapy or counseling—how various factors beyond my control influence my behavior. I may still be acting in ways that keep trying to fulfill expectations that my parents or elders ingrained in me since childhood, even though they may have long been deceased. I may catch myself doing, saying, or thinking things that are prompted by the desire to gain respect and admiration from others, or that would prove myself to be worthy of those reactions. I may also behave according to an unconscious ideal I have set for myself that has been imprinted upon me by the media, which bombards us all with images of the rich, beautiful, and famous.

Thoughts, words, and actions based on such an idealized image of myself creates the desire to have more possessions to show the world and prove to myself that I am indeed worthy. This desire to have more—whether in the form of material possessions or intellectual or spiritual assets—consumes me and drives me to act in ways that aid in their acquisition. Yet the attainment of one or another of these sought-for items never satisfies me and only whets my desire for more.

In spending my efforts and time pursuing these things I desire, I realize that I can never reach the goals I have set for myself, consciously or unconsciously. Like trying to keep pace on a treadmill that starts going faster and faster, I am never really able to catch up to where I want to be.

This condition leads to a chronic sense of insecurity and dissatisfaction with myself—with the way I live my life and the way I am—without allowing me to pinpoint the reason.

This inner sense of dissatisfaction and insecurity puts a wall between me and others around me. I tend to divide the persons around me into two camps, those who can be my allies in helping me achieve my goals and those whom I consider rivals or threats to such achievement. The latter I guard myself against, putting them at arm's length and regarding them with a certain degree of defensiveness verging on animosity or antipathy. With the former I can perhaps let my hair down a bit and enter into some kind of relationship, but only insofar as I perceive them to be useful to me and my purposes. The fact that I am not at home nor at peace within myself makes me relate to those around me in ways that are far from peaceful. I tend to regard other persons as impinging upon me, and I feel that I need to protect and defend myself against them or prove myself better or more worthy than them. Such a way of regarding other persons breeds ill will and conflict.

In this mode of living based on a false ideal of myself, which in turn engenders an inner sense of dissatisfaction and insecurity, I tend to behave in ways that only aggravate the fissure within myself and the rupture between myself and those around me. This mode of living is the breeding ground for what in the Christian tradition are described as the seven cardinal sins: greed, lust, envy, gluttony, pride, wrath, and sloth.

Greed is my way of trying to assuage that sense of insecurity and vacuity I feel in myself that needs to be filled with material possessions or intellectual and spiritual assets. Lust is what I feel toward others whom I need to use for the purposes of my own sexual or psychological satisfaction, a way of relating to another person that only widens the alienation between us. Envy is how I tend to regard another whom I perceive as having more things than I do. Gluttony is my way of wanting to gorge myself with those things I find desirable, which only further entrenches me in the patterns of addiction to things I feel that I need to prop up my insecurity. Pride is what I feel as I compare myself with others, wanting to be superior to them. Wrath is another expression for the ill will I bear toward others whom I perceive as threats to having things my way. Sloth comes from a general sense of powerlessness in attaining what I believe to be my goals, draining my energy and making me unable to take any steps toward getting out of my helpless situation.

As we continue to live our lives in the way just described, we only aggravate the sense of dissatisfaction and insecurity, propelling a vicious cycle and deepening the mire in which we find ourselves. Deep in my heart all I want is to be happy and peaceful, but I behave in ways that precisely prevent me from being truly happy and peaceful. The apostle Paul expresses this in the following way:

> I do not understand my own actions. For I do not do what I want, but I do the very thing I hate. Now if I do what I do not want, I agree that the law is good. But in fact it is no longer I that do it, but sin that dwells within me. For I know that nothing good dwells within me, that is, in my flesh. I can will what is right, but I cannot do it. For I do not do the good I want, but the evil I do not want is what I do. (Rom. 7:15–19)

This is an earnest admission, a confession of the rupture in the heart of one's being, coupled with a sense of powerlessness in not being able to do what is good as one wishes from the bottom of one's heart.

Rene Girard offers an insightful view of the human condition that resonates with Paul's statement above, in what is known as his theory of *mimetic desire*. Analyzing many literary works and reflecting on human behavior from many angles, Girard arrived at the view that we human beings are motivated in our thoughts, words, and actions by a basic desire for certain objects that is actually, consciously or unconsciously, based on what we assume others desire. This desire causes me as an individual to relate to those others whom I perceive as desiring the same things with a sense of rivalry or enmity. This mode of relating to others thus brings about conflict, tension, and envy, creating a fissure between myself and others. Taken to different levels of social relations, this situation leads to complex human dynamics that include manipulation, dissimulation, scheming against the perceived rival or enemy, and scapegoating. In this view, the human condition is defined by forces and dynamics that are beyond the control of any single human individual, which influence the individual's attitudes and behavior vis-à-vis others in mutually conflicting ways.[5]

## A Buddhist Diagnosis

In the Buddhist tradition, our human condition is described by the Pāli term *dukkha*. Often translated as "suffering," it is more aptly "a state of being ill-at-ease." The word is from a compound that means "the wheel is not aligned," "askew," or "dislocated." Its opposite is *sukha*, meaning "the wheel is well-aligned"—from the image of a wheel with the center in its proper place that rolls on smoothly—and it is translated as "happiness," "well-being," or "the state of being at ease." The dislocated wheel is the state of dissatisfaction, pain, and suffering that is our lot as we go through the cycle of birth and death, the wheel of *saṃsāra*. The well-aligned wheel is the wheel of dharma, the teaching of the Awakened

One (Buddha), which empowers us to overcome the wheel of saṃsāra and thereby enter into nirvana, a place of peace and well-being.

The acknowledgment of the state of dissatisfaction and insecurity, of not being "at ease" (dukkha), is the first of the Four Ennobling Truths taught by the Buddha. The second of these truths is the invitation to examine and root out the cause of dukkha, tracing this to the "three poisons" of greed, ill will, and ignorance. These three poisons are behind the fundamental attitude marked by craving, the root cause of our dissatisfaction and insecurity. This craving arises out of ignorance, the false image I have of myself, the illusion of what I conceive as I-me-mine that sets itself up against the rest of the world. This ignorance begets the insecurity in me that propels the mechanisms of greed, making me want to have more stuff that may make me feel a little less insecure and unworthy as I associate my identity with those things that I can have, whether material possessions or cultural, intellectual, or spiritual assets of sorts. This drive for more things to pile on to my identity makes me see others around me either as people who will help me get what I want, which makes me want to relate with them only insofar as they are useful to me; as rivals for the same things I want; or as people I can use for my purposes, which then begets ill will. In either case, the way I relate to others is marked by manipulation, rivalry, animosity, or enmity—all propelled by an insecure and deluded ego-centered consciousness.

## Three Levels of Separation

We can thus see how our individual lives are marked by separation and alienation on many levels. There is the separation between myself and my fellow human beings, from the way I relate to them either as objects of manipulation or as rivals who can potentially thwart me from getting what I want. This way of relating to those around me only aggravates my sense of alienation from them, further heightening my sense of insecurity and lack of inner peace. This alienating way of relating to one another on the level of our individual personal lives is brought to the level of social groupings, leading to a sharp divide in our consciousness marked by an attitude of us against them, based on ethnic, linguistic, geographical, cultural, social, religious, and other factors. Such attitudes are behind the situations of conflict and violence that characterize so much of our contemporary world.

There is also the sense of alienation we find between human beings and the world of nature, insofar as we look at the natural world as an object "out there" to be used and exploited for our human purposes. This attitude is at the root of the ever-worsening global ecological malaise that threatens our survival as a species on this planet.

Underlying these kinds of separation is the rift I discern within myself, as I continue to hold on to the false image of my idealized self. My inner insecurity, my dissatisfaction with myself, and ignorance of who I truly am are behind this vicious cycle that makes me relate to the world around me and to other human beings in manipulative and alienating ways.

Sin is thus best understood as a state of separation, in the different levels described. This state of separation is at the root of my dissatisfaction with myself, my insecurity, and my unhappiness, causing me to think, say, and do things that cause suffering to others as well as to myself.

How do we put a stop to this vicious cycle of dissatisfaction, insecurity, and unhappiness that characterize the way we live our lives? In short, how are we to free ourselves from the bondage of sin? To be freed from this bondage is to overcome these three levels of separation that cut right at the heart of my being—the separation between myself and other persons, the separation between myself and the world of nature, and the separation within myself; this last separation is between my true self and the false or illusory ideal of myself I have set up in my own mind.

## Original Sin and Actual Sin

A long-standing Christian tradition teaches that we human beings are born in a state of original sin. This doctrine of original sin occupies a central place in the Christian view of humanity, with differing nuances in theological understanding developed in Roman Catholic, Orthodox, and various Protestant positions. To say that this doctrine has had considerable impact on the history of Western civilization is an understatement.

The core message of this doctrine converges with the view of our human condition described above as ruptured, broken, wounded, and marked by three degrees of separation cutting us right at the heart in our lives as a global family, earth community, and individual human beings. These three degrees of separation that characterize our mode of being and underlie the sorry state of our contemporary global society constitute what we can call "the sin of the world."

Insofar as we fail to recognize this wounded state, we lead our lives in a state of ignorance. Our thoughts, words, and actions continue to issue forth from a wounded ego seeking to bolster itself and grasp onto something that would allay its anxieties and insecurities. Our lives are taken over by the three poisons of greed, ill will, and ignorance, wreaking havoc on our own life as well as the lives of others. Taking another frame of reference, the seven cardinal sins of greed, lust, envy, gluttony, pride, wrath, and sloth thereby manifest themselves in various forms in our daily lives, further damaging not only our relationships with our fellow human beings and with the natural world but our own self as well. Woundedness only begets more woundedness.

Original sin, understood as the state of alienation on various levels of our life, is what predisposes us to think, speak, and act in ways that aggravate our wounded state of being. Those thoughts, words, and actions that further cause harm and inflict suffering and pain upon ourselves, our fellow human beings, and the entire earth community are the actual sins we tend to commit under the influence of the three poisons, or of the seven cardinal sins.

The point of the First Week of the Spiritual Exercises is to awaken us to this gravely wounded and sinful state of our human condition and thereby resolve to take steps to free ourselves from it. Ignatius intends the exercises in this opening part to enable one to experience "shame and confusion upon myself," and to experience "intense sorrow and [shed] tears for my sins" (Ivens, 48). In so experiencing shame, confusion, and intense sorrow at realizing and acknowledging one's existential condition, one is moved to resolve to take steps to free oneself from this sorry state.

### Recommended Exercises for the First Week (Part I)

1. Take the daily newspaper and examine the sections on international, national, and regional news, noting the items that depict violence in different forms. After noting a particular incident and finding out the details as described, set the newspaper aside, and imagine yourself as a family member (mother, father, son, daughter, brother, sister) of one of the victims of violence. Sit and breathe in this place for half an hour.

2. Go online to www.globalissues.org and note the es-

timated number of children under five years of age who would die that day from hunger and malnutrition. Go on to survey the various items reported on the issues of global poverty, war on terror, environmental issues, and other items that draw your interest. After noting some of the items, turn your computer off, and sit and breathe in a quiet place for half an hour.

3. List some items that you use or consume on a regular basis, and trace their origins. For example, look at the label on your suit or blouse and see where it was made. If it says "Made in China," "Made in Indonesia," or "Made in El Salvador," find out more about the situation of daily laborers in those countries. Do the same with other items of regular use or daily consumption, including house or office furniture (where does the wood come from? How was it brought here?); computers (where was it assembled? Where do the parts come from?) and food and drink (coffee, sugar, chocolate, bananas, meat, fish, etc.). Ponder the intricate worldwide network that connects you with the coffee plantation workers in Brazil, the indigenous communities along the Amazon threatened with extinction with the destruction of rain forests, or the sugar plantation workers in Asia or Latin America or cacao farmers in Africa producing the material for chocolates, struggling to eke out a living for their families. Breathe in and breathe out with the awareness of sharing this breath with the countless human beings on this earth with whom we are connected in these various ways.

### Notes

[1] Ignatius invites the seeker to consider the First Sin—that is, in received narrative from early Christian tradition, the sin whereby a group of angelic beings fell into pride and rebelled against God and thereby were consigned to Hell; the Second Sin—that is, the sin of Adam and Eve, who disobeyed God's order not to touch "the fruit of the tree of

knowledge of Good and Evil," and were thus driven out of paradise; and a third kind of sin, by a human being at some point in history, who committed a mortal sin of such gravity that it condemned that person to hell for eternity. There are theological issues related to Ignatius's presentation of the three sins that we do not address here. We take a different approach toward understanding the notion of sin and its impact on our individual lives as well as in our global society.

[2]The average temperatures of our planet continue to rise. This climate change, seen as the cumulative result of many factors in which our consumer-oriented human civilization plays a central role, is leading to foreseeable catastrophic effects on our global community in the decades to come.

[3]John Paul II, *Sollicitudo Rei Socialis* (issued December 30, 1987), no. 36.

[4]Ibid., no. 37.

[5]See Rene Girard, *Violence and Desire* (Baltimore: Johns Hopkins University Press, 1978), for his development of this insight, which also underlies his other works. Girard's work calls for a more extended analysis than can be offered here.

5

# Toward Recovery

## *Turning My Life Around*

Sentient beings are numberless. I vow to free them.
Delusions are inexhaustible. I vow to end them.
(from the Four Vows of the Bodhisattva)

"Sentient being" is a term often used for all living beings, who are Buddhas right from the beginning but do not
realize it, as their eyes are blinded by delusive passions that
make them behave in ways motivated by the three poisons
of greed, ill will, and ignorance. Sentient beings thus are
shackled by these three poisons, bringing forth harmful
karma upon harmful karma in the world, causing suffering
for themselves and for everyone else. How can we be freed
from such a sorry state of being?

A deep-seated motivation that propels a person in Zen
practice is this aspiration to free not just oneself but all sentient beings from suffering and delusion. One can say that
this is also the intent of the Spiritual Exercises of St. Ignatius,
to liberate us from a life of sin and selfishness that causes
suffering for ourselves and others. The meditations on the
First Week lay bare for us the particulars of that suffering
and delusion in a rather graphic way.

These meditations confront us with our human condition in dire need of healing, a condition that lies at the root of our individual sense of alienation and dislocation as well as of the manifestly dysfunctional state of our entire human family. A straightforward look at the destructive effects wrought by our sinful and selfish ways of life especially as seen on a global scale is meant to convey to us how far we are from realizing our deepest longing as human beings— that is, to find true joy and contentment, living at peace within our hearts, with one another and with God. The First Week's meditations are not meant to leave me wallowing in guilt and shame, beating my breast and exclaiming, "Woe is me!" Rather, these meditations beckon me to turn my life around and live a life freed from the shackles of sin and selfishness, toward a life thoroughly in accord with the purpose for which I was created, as laid out in the Principle and Foundation.

With these concepts in view, the following exercises are offered in concluding the First Week: meditations on death[1] and on hell, and an overall survey of how one has lived one's life (the General Examen) up to this point. All this leads us to make a firm resolve to turn our backs on a life of sin and selfishness and whatever is the cause of suffering and delusion, and to open our hearts and entire being to a new Way.

### Meditation on Death

Meditating on death is a way of bringing us to an enhanced appreciation of the precious gift of this human life. Various forms of belief in an afterlife can be found in the different religious traditions; in many of them, biological death is regarded not so much as the final end, but rather as a passageway to the next form of life, in whatever way this might be understood. One's attitude toward death is inevitably tied up with how one conceives of the afterlife.

The fact that "I am going to die someday" is the one thing each of us can say with absolute certainty. But this fact, or the thought about it, is all too often set aside and not taken into account in the way we live our lives. The very thought of death can lead a person to react with fear, which is perhaps why the mention of death is considered taboo and avoided in polite conversation. The prevalent tendency in our contemporary consumerist culture is to sidestep the theme of death and divert the mind to various kinds of entertaining images and thoughts.

The death of a loved one, friend, or acquaintance can serve as a wakeup call, an impetus to take stock of my own death and consequently to consider the way I am living my life. Results of a medical examination indicating a death-dealing illness, like cancer, can also be an occasion that confronts me with the fact of my own impending demise and calling for a reexamination of the way I live.

The Buddha himself is said to have been launched on his path to enlightenment by his encounter with a sick person, an aging person, and finally with a corpse. In Theravada Buddhism, meditation on death is an important feature of the path to awakening. Monks and nuns are sent to graveyards to meditate and are given detailed instructions on considering the frailty and corruptibility of our mortal bodies.

"If you live each day as if it was your last, someday you'll most certainly be right." This statement, famously made by the late Apple founder and CEO, Steve Jobs, goes to the heart of the matter. In that vein, the meditation on death that Ignatius prescribes in the Spiritual Exercises poses the question, "If I were at the point of my death, or on the day of Final Judgment, how would I look back at my life, and thereby make choices in this light?"[2]

The exercise invites me to fast forward to the day of my

death, imagining it to be sometime in the unknown future and asking myself, *Is there anything in my current way of living that I would regret, or would wish I had done differently, from the vantage point of the day when I am about to die?*

This meditation on death may also take this form: *If I am told by some reliable authority that I am to die one year from today, how will I live this final year of my life? What changes in lifestyle need I make? Are there some people I need to approach, to ask forgiveness, to seek some kind of reconciliation, to say certain things to or do certain things for that I will regret not having said or done after I die? In short, are there some important things I need to take care of, so that when the time of my death comes, I will be able to meet it with equanimity?*

We can take this to a still further level, heightening the urgency and narrowing down the time frame to one month. To bring home the point in a more immediate way, the question is posed: If I had but twenty-four hours to live, how would I spend this last day of my life?

As I go through these exercises that set my own death as the vantage point for looking at my current life, I note particular items that come up on each of the levels or time frames considered and resolve to carry these out.

Going through these exercises helps me come to terms with the fact of my own impending death, whether it may come tomorrow, one month from today, one year from today, or even ten, twenty, thirty, or more years from now. It sets my life in perspective and empowers me to make certain decisions that may turn my life around, from a way of life that takes things for granted and assumes that things will go on the way it does until who knows when, to one that welcomes what each day brings with deep gratitude and appreciates the gifts that life brings day by day, moment by moment.

I am reminded of something I read in one of our required spiritual books as a Jesuit novice, recounting incidents in the life of a monk who later became a canonized saint. In one of these, this monk was playing *pelota* (a kind of ball game) with fellow monks during their afternoon recreation time, when he was asked, "Brother, if you were told that you were to die one hour from now, what would you do?" This saintly monk replied, "Why, I would continue playing *pelota*, what else? And then, after we finish with the game, I would take my bath and change, and then go and help in the kitchen, as that is my assignment for this afternoon." In short, this monk was at peace with himself, the world, and God. He was living his life in this way, ready to meet his death at any point along the way.

The exercises of the First Week are meant to prepare each of us to be able to live like this, rejoicing and relishing every moment of our life, and ready to meet our death whenever it comes, with no regrets whatsoever.

## Meditation on Hell

Ignatius includes a meditation on hell in the First Week as a graphic way of bringing home the horrors wrought by human sinfulness, and thus inspiring and bolstering one's resolve to want to avoid it at all costs. The notion of hell is by no means a Christian monopoly. The Jewish Scriptures refer to *sheol*, where the dead are consigned. Muslims believe in hell as one of their articles of faith. Buddhist cosmology consists of a tenfold realm of beings, with the realm of Buddhas at the top, followed in descending order by three levels of Buddhist saints and heavenly beings, with human beings on the fifth rung, followed by four lower realms, the realm of hell being at the very bottom. This realm is populated by beings who are enclosed within their own egocentric worlds and who have shut off all contact with others, a lonely world seeped in pain, suffering, and frustration. The Buddhist hell, however, is not a permanent one, and an individual being's consignment to hell is ended when the harmful karma that caused one to be sent there in the first place is exhausted.

Many of our contemporaries may no longer take serious images of hellfire and brimstone to which the damned are consigned after death, but the notion of hell as a consequence of the evil and harmful acts perpetrated by freely acting human beings calls for a review. Reflecting on our human experience conveys to us the fact that hell does exist and is closer to us than we think. A look at our recent history over the last century—with two world wars and many more armed conflicts on regional scale; the Shoah perpetrated by Hitler's Nazi regime; the gulags of the Stalinist Soviet Union; the cultural revolution of Mao Zedong's China; the killing fields of Pol Pot's Cambodia; the Rwandan massacres; the genocidal conflicts in various regions; the ongoing Israeli-Palestinian conflict; Iraq and Afghanistan; and so many conflicts based on ethnic, political, social, and other factors that have set humans against one another—all reveal a hellish scenario indeed.

Our contemporary scene, with ongoing violence being perpetrated on so many different level—including the structural violence toward the twenty-one thousand children under the age of five who die daily of malnutrition and related causes; the military violence invoked in declared and undeclared wars in various regions of the world; the physical violence against the most vulnerable, especially women and children; the psychological violence characterizing many kinds of human relationships, and so on—bring home to us the fact that we humans are capable of making hell on this very earth.

For those who have had the opportunity to visit memorials at Auschwitz, Dachau, Treblinka, and others; the Holocaust Memorial Museum in Washington, DC; the Killing Fields Museum in Phnom Penh, Cambodia; or other places commemorating horrific acts perpetrated by human beings upon one another, a most natural and spontaneous reaction is that of a cold shudder, a sense of shock that human beings can be capable of such heinous acts against fellow human beings. A voice that comes forth from the depths for those who sit and contemplate such hellish situations is enshrined in the cry, "Never again!" This resolve wells up in many human beings, to live in a way that one will not allow members of our global family to ever experience such horrible situations again.

Leaving this somber scenario in the background, I am reminded of a fable I read in a Japanese storybook. This story assumes a traditional view of the afterlife, wherein the souls of human beings who pass on from this earthly life, based on how they lived that life, are destined either to a place of true happiness, "heaven," or a place of damnation and suffering, "hell."

While waiting in line for judgment, a soul is approached by an angel who offers to guide it on a tour of those two "places of final destination." First, being led through a dark tunnel, the soul is ushered into a big hall where many hungry souls are gathered around a big table with all kinds of delicious food waiting to be eaten. Around the table are chopsticks of about a meter in length. The signal is given for mealtime, and these poor hungry souls rush forward to eat, but the rule is that they must use those long chopsticks to feed themselves. They all try to put the food into their mouths using these long chopsticks, but alas, the tip of the chopsticks holding the food cannot reach their mouth due to the length of the sticks. They keep on trying, but they only get more frustrated as the food that each one tries to grab from the table and put into one's own mouth keeps dropping to the floor. "What a frustrating scene indeed," the soul bemoans. This must really be hell, having what you want right in front of you, but you cannot partake of it—a state of eternal unhappiness and frustration.

"Take me to the other place," the soul begs the angel. "Maybe the chopsticks there are not so long." The angel obliges, and they enter another large hall, decked with similar tables of delicious food, also with many hungry souls around the table waiting for the signal to start eating. Our soul on tour looks closely and checks the chopsticks, only to see that they are just as long as those in the other place. The signal is given, and the hungry souls approach the table, taking the long chopsticks to begin eating. But in this case, instead of just trying to put the food into their own mouths, the souls here begin by taking food with the chopsticks and offering it to one another. "Hmm, this looks good. Try this!" "Ah, thank you. Here, let me offer you this in return." The souls on this side use the long chopsticks to offer the food to one another and partake of a convivial feast, expressing gratitude to one another as they go on in eternal celebration.

The point of the story is simple. The difference between heaven and hell lies in the turn of the heart that we human beings are capable of taking in this life—the turn from a selfish attitude that marks a life centered on egoistic pursuits to an attitude of openness and generosity that marks a life of selfless service to others and gratitude for the gifts of the earth. What kind of world would it be if each and every inhabitant of this earth lived in this way! Just imagine!

### Spotlight on My Life: The Examen

In an exercise called the General Examen, Ignatius recommends combing through one's entire life to identify those instances wherein one has harbored thoughts, uttered words, or engaged in actions harmful to oneself and to others, so that one may recognize and acknowledge one's sins, truly experience sorrow and shame for them, and thereby be strengthened in the resolve not to repeat them. Requiring courage and determination, this exercise is meant to shed light on every nook and cranny of one's entire life, highlighting those features that one would rather not recall or that may cause one to feel pangs of regret, repentance, or even shame. Undertaking this exercise can lead to a refreshing experience of inner cleansing, disposing the exercitant to live from this point on with a totally different attitude of mind and heart.[3]

This exercise of examining one's entire life begins with an act of thanksgiving for all the blessings one has received throughout one's life since birth up to this point.[4] Rather than simply going through this opening part in a perfunctory way and then moving on to emphasize the sinful side of one's past, taking time here to truly comb through one's entire life and recall those things for which one can truly be grateful can make a difference in the way we were able to appreciate our own life and the gifts thereof. Launching on this exercise with a sense of deep gratitude for all the blessings in my life will also heighten my sense of sorrow and regret as I see and acknowledge those times when I caused harm to others and to myself.

By seeing the brokenness of our human condition on a global scale, and tracing the causes of this global woundedness to the way we live our lives as individuals mired in sin and selfishness, we are given a clue as to where the path to recovery may lie. We see through the three poisons of greed, ill will, and delusion, overturning them with their antidotes: generosity, goodwill, and wisdom.

The First Week of the Spiritual Exercises is meant to

make us shudder at the thought of continuing to live a life wallowing in selfishness and sin, and to seek a turn toward a new life liberated from the shackles of sin. Ignatius provides the setting for us to deepen this resolution and make it truly operative in our lives: "Repent, and believe in the good news" (Mark 1:15).

### Recommended Exercises for the First Week (Part 2)

1. Meditation on death: As described above, imagine yourself at your deathbed and look at your present life from that vantage point (see above for particulars).

2. Meditation on hell: Recall the current state of our world in need of healing (as described in the last chapter) and imagine a world that is not like that: where people care for one another, we live our lives in harmony with the natural world, and each individual lives in peace and contentment. Ask yourself, *How can I live my own life in a way that I can help bring about such a world?*

3. General Examen (Part 1): Sit in a quiet place in a comfortable position, and be aware as you breathe in and out. Maintain this awareness with each breath. As you do, recall the individuals in your life who have showered you with love and affection, beginning with biological or foster parents (recall each separately), grandparents, uncles or aunts and other relatives, teachers, benefactors, and friends. Stay with each individual for a sufficient time to be able to appreciate the support and love they gave to you and continue to give you, wherever they may be at this point, whether deceased or still living. Acknowledge this with gratitude, addressing the particular individuals as if each were present before you with words you wish to convey to them.

4. General Examen (Part 2): Recall individuals in your life, since your childhood and on through youth and into

adulthood, who may have harmed or hurt you or caused you pain and suffering in particular ways. Place one of them before you in your mind and watch the emotions that well up as you do. Again in your mind's eye, say what you wish to say to this person who has played the role of one who has hurt you or caused you suffering. During this time, breathe deeply with awareness of each in-breath and out-breath, and note the fact that this person before you in your mind's eye is also breathing, in and out. Put yourself in the place of that person you are considering in this way, imagining that person's sentiments, thoughts, attitudes, and view of the world. Imagine what this person would say to you in response to what you have just conveyed to him or her. Sit in silence and breathe with awareness through the process.

5. General Examen (Part 3): Recall the events of your life, beginning with your childhood, wherein you may have done things that hurt other persons around you. Focus on the place, the situation, the persons involved, and what you thought, said, or did that caused that hurt. Sit and breathe attentively and put yourself in the position of those persons you hurt. Imagine where they are now, and what you would say to them now as you recall those incidents. Move on to another event or situation and imagine the same. End the session by imagining those persons before you, and asking forgiveness of each one you may have hurt in those different ways you are able to recall.

### Notes

[1]The meditation on death is not specifically listed among the exercises of the First Week, but seasoned spiritual directors include this as a way of bolstering the desired fruit of the First Week, that is, a change of heart on the part of the exercitant. See Karl Rahner, *Spiritual Exercises* (New York: Herder and Herder, 1965), 89–92.

[2]See Ignatius's text for "the second method for making a wise and good choice" (Anthony Mottola, *The Spiritual Exercises of St. Ignatius* [New York: Image Books, 1964], 86).

[3]At this point Ignatius recommends the Sacrament of Penance, which in Roman Catholic tradition is the penitential rite of confessing one's sins to a priest who acts as the representative of God.

[4]"The first point is to give thanks to God for the benefits I have received" (Mottola, *Spiritual Exercises*, 53).

# PART THREE

# *ILLUMINATION*

A seeker enters the stage of illumination as he or she begins to get little glimpses confirming that one has taken the right direction in one's life. In Zen, as one settles in to a sustained practice of sitting on a regular basis and finding inner peace and joy in just being still, finding oneself better able to pay attention to the here and now and enjoying the fruits of concentration that is a mark of this practice, such glimpses can come in unguarded moments. They may be on the level of intellectual insights that clarify for us some important things about our life, or they may come from a deeper level, whereby we are opened to an experiential realization that sheds light on the question, "Who am I?" The latter is called "seeing one's true nature," a pivotal experience in the Zen path.

In the Ignatian Spiritual Exercises, after one has undergone the purificatory process entailed in the First Week, the Second Week is ushered in with an invitation to fix our gaze on Jesus, who opens us to the Way, illuminating our path with his own life in his words and actions. We devote the fifth and eighth chapters to this task. In this Second Week, Ignatius also introduces exercises that help the seeker clarify *important elements in one's life, and to ground one in making choices that are in accordance with the Way. The sixth and seventh chapters consider these items as aspects of the stage of Illumination.*

# 6

# Let Me Know the Way

## *Contemplating Jesus*

The third and fourth lines of the Four Vows of the Bodhisattva read as follows:

Dharma Gates are boundless. I vow to enter them.
The enlightened Way is unsurpassable. I vow to
    embody it.

To embody this peerless enlightened Way in one's entire
life, 24/7, in all that one thinks, says, and does is the aspiration as well as the great resolve of the Zen practitioner.
The vow to enter all the dharma gates freely and be able to
master the dharma goes hand in hand with this aspiration.

Acknowledging one's need of healing and having resolved
to turn one's life in this direction, one is now ready for the
next stage: Illumination.

The Second Week of the Spiritual Exercises guides the
seeker to better understand, appreciate, and embody the
Way in one's own life. We begin this stage with a thorough
resolve to turn our back on the path of self-centered habits
that only lead to harm and destruction, and instead devote
our entire life in seeking to do only what is in accordance

with the purpose for which we were created. How may I know this as it applies in particular to my own individual life? How may I know the Way?

Ignatius begins the Second Week with a meditation on the kingdom of Christ. The point of this exercise is to solidify our Great Resolve to live a new Way of life under the leadership of Christ the King, challenging us to a spirit of self-sacrifice, magnanimity, and generosity of heart. For Ignatius the soldier, who had given his loyalties to the Duke of Navarre up to the time he was wounded in battle, this was a particularly significant exercise, in making a transfer of loyalties from an earthly king to Christ the King.

While this feature of the Ignatian Exercises has been well known, for various reasons that include what is explained below, we forgo this particular exercise and begin our entry into the Second Week by considering the Great Resolve, as the monk displays in the following case example:

> A monk asked Jōshū (Zhao-zhou) in all earnestness, "Master, I have just entered the monastery. Now please show me the Way." Jōshū asked, "Have you eaten your rice gruel?" The monk replied, "Yes, Master." Jōshū said, "Then go and wash your bowls." (*Gateless Gate*, no. 7)

The monk here has abandoned his former life of self-seeking ambition and is now ready to take on a spiritual path of awakening. We can touch on many aspects to highlight the importance of this koan in the context of Zen practice,[1] but we focus here on only two points. First, the monk's resolve is strong and clear. His having entered a monastery to seek the Way itself speaks to that. Second, in response, after having been assured that the monk's basic needs are met (having had his rice gruel, etc.), the Zen master's instruction is "Go and wash your bowls"—that is, cleanse yourself of everything that is an obstacle to the way in your past life and come with a fresh slate, with an open mind and heart.

Taking the Chinese context in which this exchange occurred, the Way as rendered in English refers to the Tao (Dao), a central notion in East Asian culture and religion. In brief, the Tao can be understood as the Way of the universe, the Way of nature, as well as the Way of human beings in living a fully authentic life.[2] In short, it is the Ultimate Way that is also the very concrete Way as manifested in our day-to-day life on earth. As Buddhism took root and blossomed in China, this notion of the Way came to be associated with the Enlightened Way, the Way of Awakening, or the Way of the Buddhas. We use the term here with all these nuances in mind.

The First Week of the Exercises was precisely about "washing our bowls," so at this point we are ready to enter into the Second Week. Ignatius invites us to fix our gaze on Jesus, who will show us the Way. We are now about to enter the main segment of the Exercises: contemplative practice on aspects of the life of Jesus, based on scriptural accounts in the New Testament.

### A Note on Reading Scriptures

Before proceeding, a note on various ways that sacred texts have been read in some of the world's religious traditions would be helpful.

The Jewish tradition has a fourfold level of reading Scriptures, distinguishing the literal, allegorical, homiletical, and mystical ways of approaching the sacred text. The first has to do with the philological, literary, historical, sociological, and contextual aspects that make up the written word. The Hebrew/Aramaic term for this approach is *p'shat*, meaning "plain" or "simple." A second level of approach is a figurative, metaphorical, allegorical, or symbolic way of reading, wherein concrete things or events are read in ways that point to something else they are taken to represent. The Hebrew/Aramaic term for this is *remez*, meaning "hint."

A third level takes the sacred text as material for homiletical purposes, drawing out the implications for human behavior, specifically ethical action. The term for this is *d'rash*, meaning "to inquire" or "to seek" in Hebrew. The fourth level has to do with the "secret" (*sod* in Hebrew) or "mystical" meaning of the text, which opens the reader to a new dimension of understanding not only of the text itself but also of oneself in relation to the world, the text, and to everything else.[3]

Christian tradition offers the "four senses of Scripture," roughly corresponding to the levels described in the Jewish way of reading above, differentiating the first—literal or "material"—level from the next three "spiritual" ways of reading. The latter three are about levels of meaning inspired by the Holy Spirit. Since early times these different ways of reading and interpreting sacred Scriptures have informed Christians, serving as the basis for spiritual life, moral judgment and behavior, and theological and pastoral reflection. Contrasting approaches can be seen in the Alexandrian school on the one hand—which emphasized the allegorical method, with Clement of Alexandria and Origen as major figures—and in the Antioch school on the other, which emphasized the literal level of interpretation, with the golden-tongued preacher St. John Chrysostom as a renowned representative.

Other religious traditions have developed ways in which faithful adherents read, understand, and appropriate their own sacred texts into their life and behavior.[4] Debates among scholars on the various ways of interpreting sacred texts toward opening the mind of wisdom in the realization of the ultimate constitute a significant part of Hindu commentarial literature.[5]

Over centuries of Buddhist history, strategies for reading its scriptural texts developed as ways that informed spiritual practice toward awakening. Scriptural texts, known as sutras or "threads of wisdom," were received and read as ways of reconnecting with the Awakened One. These revered texts, each beginning with the phrase "Thus I have heard," were composed over a span of more than a thousand years by scribes who themselves were able to enter into the awakened state and are considered by followers as the authoritative word of the Buddha himself.[6]

Nichiren, a thirteenth-century Japanese Buddhist figure whose influence remains strong today, offers what is known as a "bodily reading of the Lotus Sutra," which reads the scriptural text vis-à-vis contemporary events, drawing forth a reader's embodied engagement with those events from the salvific standpoint of the Lotus Sutra.[7]

Acknowledging inspiration from Nichiren's bodily reading of the Lotus Sutra as well as from his own Zen practice, Fr. Kakichi Kadowaki, Jesuit priest and authorized Zen master in the Rinzai (Linji) tradition, proposes a "body-reading" (*shindoku*) of Christian scriptural text, wherein the reader is not a mere spectator or outside observer but is drawn existentially into the world of the text and becomes a key participant.[8]

In sum, religious traditions of the world uphold as sacred their own set of Scriptures, that is, written texts having spiritual and transformative power for the members of the community that regards them as such. In our contemporary globalized society, the spiritual treasures of the many diverse religious communities that thrive in their respective locales all over the world are readily made accessible not just to the adherents of those communities but to outsiders as well.

For example, an outsider to the Hindu tradition (it could be a Christian, Muslim, Jew, Buddhist, Sikh, or atheist, to name some examples) may turn to the Upanishads or to the Bhagavad Gita and, with an open and earnest mind, encounter something therein that is spiritually powerful and transformative. Or it could be Buddhist Scriptures like the Heart Sutra or Lotus Sutra, or the Psalms or the Qur'an, that an outsider to the religious tradition of those particular scriptural texts may approach and experience something to that effect. The capacity to bring about such spiritually transformative and nourishing moments in those who approach them openly may be referred to as the "revelatory power" of those scriptural texts.[9]

In this context we can turn to New Testament scriptural texts, offering them not just for the insiders from the Christian tradition who hold these texts as sacred and revealed but for all earnest spiritual seekers who might also encounter something powerful and transformative in them for their own lives.

As recent biblical scholarship has cogently shown, New Testament writings, specifically the four Gospels (Matthew, Mark, Luke, and John), are not to be taken as historical accounts but as narratives coming forth from the faith of the early Christian community that emerged after the death of Jesus, whom they referred to as the Christ (Anointed One) of God. They are a testimony of the faith of the followers of this itinerant Jewish teacher, who preached to them good news of the coming of the reign of God in their midst, and in whose presence they experienced an encounter with a Holy Mystery.

The New Testament narratives and passages we take up as the theme of our contemplative practice—focusing on the events around Jesus as well as his words and actions—may thus also serve for us as a locus for an encounter with Mystery.

### Toward Interior Knowledge: Taste and See

Ignatius gives us detailed guidelines in approaching Scripture for contemplative exercises with what he calls "application of the senses." By this the active imagination is brought in to see, hear, smell, taste, touch, and imagine particular items surrounding a given scriptural scene. All this is geared toward an interior knowledge of the heart of Jesus Christ, so as to be able to live and embody the Way in this spirit. We are ushered into the heart of Jesus. In concrete terms, our intent is to be able to see, hear, smell, taste, touch, and think as he did, that one may be able to exclaim, with the apostle Paul, "It is no longer I who live, but it is Christ who lives in me" (Gal. 2:20).

Reading the scriptural text in a way that engages all the senses, including imagination, is our mode of approach. Scriptural passages we consider are invitations for us to taste and see Jesus in action, in the context of his discourses and encounters with disciples and others who were part of his world.

To contemplate is to behold, to set our gaze upon, and to allow ourselves to bask in the light of what we are contemplating. In each of the passages considered here, the intended fruit is interior knowledge. As one becomes familiar and more deeply intimate with the world revealed in the text, one may experience a "fusion of horizons." This is a "personal existential affair in which one imagines the story of Jesus within one's own story."[10]

This fusion of horizons means that we see with the eyes and hear with the ears of Jesus, breathe the same air as Jesus, and feel our hearts throb in the same beat as the heart of Jesus. And lo and behold, the Way opens!

In examining passages from the New Testament as our

way of encountering and entering into the heart of Jesus, a question looms in the back of our minds as we engage in these exercises, seeking illumination: "What is the Way?" Asking the question in an up-close-and-personal manner, "How may I embody the Way in my own life?"

Having outlined the key features of our approach, we are now ready to enter into the exercises of the Second Week. In the text of the Exercises, Ignatius himself provides key passages of important events in the life of Jesus, and he includes an appendix with additional passages that individual practitioners may also take up on their own.

## A Child is Born to Us (Luke 2:1–14)

In those days a decree went out from Emperor Augustus that all the world should be registered. This was the first registration and was taken while Quirinius was governor of Syria. All went to their own towns to be registered. Joseph also went from the town of Nazareth in Galilee to Judea, to the city of David called Bethlehem, because he was descended from the house and family of David. He went to be registered with Mary, to whom he was engaged and who was expecting a child. While they were there, the time came for her to deliver her child. And she gave birth to her firstborn son and wrapped him in bands of cloth, and laid him in a manger, because there was no place for them in the inn. In that region there were shepherds living in the fields, keeping watch over their flock by night. An angel of the Lord stood before them, and the glory of the Lord shone around them, and they were terrified. But the angel said to them, "Do not be afraid; for see—I am bringing you good news of great joy for all the people: to you is born this day in the city of David a Savior, who is the Messiah, the Lord. This will be a sign for you: you will find a child wrapped in bands of cloth and lying in a manger." And suddenly there was with the angel a multitude of the heavenly host, praising God and saying, "Glory to God in the highest heaven, and on earth peace among those whom he favors!"

For Christians throughout the world, a Christmas crèche with Joseph and Mary at the stable gazing at the baby Jesus laid in a manger, with donkeys, horses, sheep, and other household animals around them and shepherds coming to pay tribute to the newborn, is a familiar scene. It is found in family altars, department store show windows, and town plaza displays during Christmas season every year. It is a scene of joy, celebration, and thanksgiving, accompanied by singing of carols and hymns, echoing the phrase, "Glory to God in the highest heaven, and on earth peace among those whom he favors!" (Luke 2:14)

Even for many who are not believing Christians but live in areas where Christian influence is dominant or at least a visible feature of the cultural landscape, setting up a Christmas crèche is taken not so much as an expression of religious belief but rather as a celebratory custom of the season. In Japan, for example, where Christians number less than 1 percent of the total population, department stores, shopping malls, and other public areas have taken the custom of displaying a Christmas crèche and of playing Christmas carols, sometimes even from early November through late December. This may be much like what the American celebration of Thanksgiving has become for people in other parts of the world, many of whom may have never been to the United States and have never heard of the historical background of this feast.

The question for us is how this scene of the birth of Jesus, as described in the Gospel of Luke, can speak to the wider human community beyond the Christian fold. Let's take the first cue from Ignatius, who recommends applying the senses as we contemplate this nativity scene. As you settle into the silence, put the scene in your mind's eye. Look at the newborn baby, Jesus, sleeping peacefully in the manger. Look up and behold the face of Mary, gentle and graceful, with a heart filled with joy and hope. Turn your gaze to Joseph, proud and joyful as well, yet also with some apprehension as to how to go on from here.

The birth of a child is a profoundly moving human experience, as anyone who has assisted or been present at a birthing can attest. A newborn child always draws us to itself and elicits a smile. Something is touched in our very depths in an encounter with a newborn, connecting us with something of goodness, innocence, beauty, and grace. Recall that we, too, without exception, were newborn once. We can partake deep within us of that primal goodness, innocence, beauty, and grace that this particular newborn child embodies and also evokes in us. Let us sit and breathe quietly and allow this concept to sink in.

I recall two separate occasions, fifteen months apart at the same Baylor Hospital in Dallas, Texas: the precious moments when our two sons, Florian and Benjamin, were born. Maria and I were delirious with joy for days, although Maria still had to go through the discomforting postnatal period that is part of the process. In my case, going back to school to prepare for classes, I was in such a daze and so ecstatic that I could not do anything but walk around campus for hours, just drinking in the joy. Contemplating the nativity scene, one can feel the joy that Joseph and Mary must have felt on this occasion.

I recall another instance of gazing at a child, a moment that remains imprinted in my heart. I was sitting on the back steps of the hospital run by the Missionary Sisters of Charity founded by Mother Teresa in Calcutta, India. As a newly ordained Jesuit priest, I was visiting there for a week with the intention of helping out with the work of the sisters. I joined them in various tasks, including going around the city in a van looking for people who were lying on the streets—there were many in Calcutta—to see if they needed medical help. If so, we would carry them into the van and take them to the hospital for treatment. I was also glad and honored to have been invited to offer the morning Eucharist with the sisters' community several times that week.

One early evening, having finished the work of the day, I was relaxing after dinner on the cement steps at the back of the hospital building. The sisters had the daily custom of taking all the leftover food after the patients had been fed to the back of the hospital, offering it to whoever would come and take it. In this time, many refugees had flocked to the city of Calcutta from the north due to a famine that was raging in that region. A group of them—men and women of various ages, families with children—were lining up to receive the leftover food from Mother Teresa's hospital pantry. After receiving their share of food, people would walk over to a suitable place in the vicinity where they could sit down and eat. Some were sitting in groups on the ground chatting away, and others were eating alone.

A few feet in front of me I noticed a little boy seated on a brick, not more than three years old, in a tattered shirt and with bare feet. He was carefully dipping bread into his pea soup in a tin can that he used for a food container. As he was doing so, he happened to look up at me with his big, dark eyes, with a half-smile showing his contentment at having a meal for the night. My first kneejerk reaction was a fuzzy emotion of pity with a twinge of guilt, seeing this poor little boy with no home and no certain future and looking at myself in contrast, with all the privileges and advantages of my position in life. As my gaze met those big, dark eyes and his half-smile, I spontaneously smiled back and started to make a funny face to make the boy laugh. I could not speak his language nor he mine, but for a few moments we exchanged funny gestures and kept looking and smiling at one another in playful nonverbal banter. In the midst of doing so, I felt the barriers between us—age, language, culture, social situation, present and future prospects, all that separated me, a young Jesuit priest not quite thirty who was visiting here from Japan where I worked, and this little three-year-old refugee boy from northern India—dissolve into nothing. Suddenly it was just that moment of play and laughing heartily. And we did. At that moment, something from deep within me welled up, and I can only offer fumbling and words here to describe what it was: *It is OK. He is taken care of.*

Almost forty years have passed since that moment. Could he have died of starvation in the next wave of famine that affected his family and people; or of some illness aggravated by malnutrition; or by accident, being run over by a car in the busy streets of Calcutta? Did he grow up and get into trouble with the law? Or did he go to school, find a job, help support his family, get married and have children, and live a middle-class life? I will never know. But that voice that welled up in that moment of encounter, of communion, is still clearly audible to me: *It is OK. He is taken care of.* In moments of stillness and clarity, that voice reassures me, *It is OK. You are also taken care of.*

Here I offer reflections from a Christian perspective, and I invite those who are open to it to listen in. Needless to say, Christians regard the event of Jesus' birth as the momentous salvific event in history wherein God "became flesh and lived among us" (John 1:4). Christians take the Hebrew word *Immanuel* [God-with-us] to mean not only that the invisible and transcendent God is present to us in a spiritual way but that God has literally become one of us: human, weak, vulnerable, capable of suffering and pain—just like us in all things (except for sin), embodied in this newborn child, Jesus. And to recall a theological doctrine that is central to the Eastern Orthodox Christian tradition but that has unfortunately been somewhat downplayed in Western Christianity, God became human in order for the human to become divine. This is our ultimate destiny: being fully one with Divinity. This momentous event of God becoming human (called the incarnation) has opened the Way to the human becoming divine (*theosis* in Greek). How? Christian teaching tells us to look at Jesus and follow him.

Let us take this birth scene as one locus for looking at and following Jesus as our Way to the Divine. The moment of Jesus' birth lifts up the birth of every human being here on earth, since time immemorial until the end of time, as a divine event, to be celebrated and welcomed as such. It also affirms the infinite worth of every human life born on this earth, revealing to us our divine origin and ultimate destiny: we are all called to the fullness of communion in the divine life.

The heart of the Christian gospel message can be summed up in this way. It is good news indeed, which each one of us is invited to hear and accept: You are called to a divine destiny. Open your heart and receive the good news!

Thomas Merton, in a well-cited account in his journal of March 19, 1958, describes an event whereby he was graced with a glimpse of this destiny:

> Yesterday, at Louisville, at the corner of Fourth and Walnut, suddenly realized that I loved all the people, and that none of them were or could be totally alien to me. As if waking up from a dream—the dream of my

separateness, of the "special" vocation to be different. My vocation does not really make me different from the rest of men, or put me in a special category except artificially, juridically. I am still a member of the human race, and what more glorious destiny is there for man, since the Word was made flesh and became, too, a member of the Human Race!

Thank God! Thank God! I am only another member of the human race, like all the rest of them. I have the immense joy of being a man! As if the sorrows of our condition could really matter, once we begin to realize who and what we are—as if we could ever begin to realize it on earth. . . .

God is seen and reveals himself as a man, that is, in us, and there is no other hope of finding wisdom than in God-manhood: our own manhood transformed in God![11]

Merton edited this entry in his journal and included it in his *Conjectures of a Guilty Bystander*:

I have the immense joy of being man, a member of a race in which God Himself became incarnate. As if the sorrows and stupidities of the human condition could overwhelm me, now I realize what we all are. And if only everybody could realize this! But it cannot be explained. There is no way of telling people that they are all walking around shining like the sun. . . . Then it was as if I suddenly saw the secret beauty of their hearts, the depths of their hearts, where neither sin nor desire nor self-knowledge can reach, the core of their reality, the person that each one is in God's eyes. If only they could all see themselves as they re-

ally are. If only we could see each other that way all
the time.[12]

In that blessed moment, Thomas Merton was given a glimpse
of the divine spark in every human person, a flint waiting
to be kindled to its full brightness.

Gazing contemplatively at the newborn child Jesus, we
see the face of every newborn child on earth. Conversely, in
the face of every newborn child is the face of Jesus. And in
the stillness of this contemplative moment in gazing at the
child, in a moment of grace, we may also be given a glimpse
of that wondrous sight that Merton was given to behold.
At the same time, we may also be able to hear a voice from
the depths, addressed to the child, as it is to each and every
one of us: *It is OK. You are taken care of.*

This voice is not unlike the voice that Jesus himself, grown
and coming to John the Baptist to be baptized at the Jordan
River, heard from the heavens: "You are my Son, the Beloved; with you I am well pleased" (Mark 1:11). If we listen
intently and earnestly in the stillness, we also may be able
to hear that voice from within, addressed to each of us, to
every human being—man, woman, and child—in our own
unique and particular way: *You are my beloved, in whom
I am well pleased.*

This same voice reverberates throughout the cosmos as
we gaze at this child in the manger, sleeping peacefully under
the watchful eyes of Joseph and Mary. *It is OK. He is taken
care of. This is my Beloved, in whom I am well pleased.*
Given all that this child is to go through later in his life—in
his daily life with his parents as he was growing up, in his
launching of his public ministry proclaiming the good news,
and eventually in his arrest, torture, public humiliation, and
ignominious death on the cross as a condemned criminal

of the Roman Empire. .... *This is my Beloved, in whom I am well pleased.*

Again I recall the boy I met in the backstreets of Calcutta. Whatever happened to him I will never know, yet that voice I heard at that moment of encounter assures me, *It is OK. He is taken care of.* And so am I.

Back to the scene of Jesus' birth: let's consider now the situation of Joseph and Mary, not unlike the situation of countless individuals and families in our world today: there is "no place for them at the inn." Millions of people are displaced from their ancestral homes due to economic, political, social, and other factors, and they find themselves as displaced persons, refugees, or undocumented aliens, discriminated against in various ways. Breathe in, breathe out, and holding each one of these countless brothers and sisters in my heart, a voice wells up, *I am that.*

I offer here for you "A Christmas Story" by David Maldonado Jr.:

> The young couple grabbed what they could carry with them and set out in the dark night. They were leaving familiar surroundings, as well as their home, friends, and family. They were expecting their firstborn and wished the child could be born at home surrounded by their community. But for the sake of the child, the young couple knew they must leave, so they walked out into the cold and dangerous desert night. It was a huge risk for them to leave, but it was also a leap of faith and hope that the land to which they were going would be a life-saving and life-sustaining place.
>
> As they made their way through the darkness, guided only by a sea of brilliant stars, they wondered what their future held for them and their child. It was their hope for the child that kept them focused and determined on

their trek. They were afraid. Robbers were known to attack travelers in the night and in the desert. What if they were caught in the night? Would they be arrested and treated as common criminals? Would they be sent back to their homeland?

Fears have a way of immobilizing some people. But for this young expectant couple, fear drove them even deeper into the night. What they feared the most would be life without hope, life without a future for their new family. In their whispers they encouraged each other and prayed that their child be born in the new land of hope. They had to arrive in their new land before day broke.

But that was not to be. The child could no longer wait to be born. They were now well into their new land. They knew no one here and their surroundings looked strange and foreign. Where could they go for the birth of their child? Who would welcome them and offer hospitality? They knocked on the first door that they saw. The lights were on and the house looked welcoming. They saw the curtains move, and a face peeked out to see who was knocking on the door. But the door did not open. From outside the house, they heard the voice of a woman inside.

"Who is it?" she asked in a whisper. A male voice from within the house responded in a loud irritated voice as if wanting to be heard by the travelers standing outside the door.

"Oh, nobody, just some foreigners probably looking for a handout," responded the male voice, adding, "They should go back to where they came from."

The young couple, hearing the voices, covered their heads and kept going. They were determined to survive. They came to yet another house with its lights still on.

"Maybe they will be more welcoming," cried the young pregnant woman. This time, the door opened slightly.

"Who are you? What do you want? Where are you from?" the voice called from within the slightly opened door.

"We just arrived and our child is ready to be born," responded the young father-to-be. "We are not from here. We are not asking for charity. All we need is for our child to be born safely. I am willing to work to repay you for your kindness."

"Humph! Some more of them. They just cause problems for the rest of us. I wish they would stop coming. I wish they would just leave. Our whole town is changing because of them, but I could sure use his cheap labor in the morning. They are good workers. Hope nobody is looking," thought the man from behind the door.

With a suspicious glare, the man yelled out, "OK, you can stay in the back, but don't make trouble or we will call the police on you and send you back where you came from."

And so the child is born in a new land, a child born of humble immigrants who seek nothing more than life and hope for tomorrow. Many of us know this as the story of the birth of Jesus. It is also the story of the birth of the child of the immigrant today.[13]

The above are some sample reflections on the scene of the birth of Jesus, following Ignatius's directions in applying the senses of sight, hearing, smell, taste, touch, and imagination to the passage being considered. I have offered reflective pointers based on this scene at some length, given its significance not only for Christians but, as hinted at above, for all of us as human beings of goodwill, who are open to new horizons of understanding and appreciating this gift of being human.

Now I invite the reader to find time to sit in silence in a comfortable spot, reread the passage in Luke's Gospel above, follow the same guidelines for contemplation, and launch off on your own. An added suggestion would be to keep a journal and jot down whatever comes up in those times of contemplative silence. These suggested instructions apply, too, for the rest of the contemplative exercises in this book.

### Ordinary Mind Is the Way: The Early Life of Jesus (Luke 2:39–40, 51–52)

> When they had finished everything required by the law of the Lord, they returned to Galilee, to their own town of Nazareth. The child grew and became strong, filled with wisdom; and the favor of God was upon him. . . . Then he went down with them and came to Nazareth, and was obedient to them. His mother treasured all these things in her heart. And Jesus increased in wisdom and in years, and in divine and human favor.

These passages give a summary account of Jesus' infancy, childhood, youth, and young adulthood, until the launching of his public life of teaching and proclaiming the coming of the reign of God. Other than these few sentences, one finds little in reliable written sources about the early life of Jesus. Much is left to speculation.[14] In contemplating the various events in the early life of Jesus, we use Ignatius's method of application of the senses, precisely including the imagination, as a creative way of placing ourselves within the scene and enabling a fusion of horizons to occur.

We imagine the infant smiling, giggling, and growing up in the loving care of his mother and father. Toddler gradually takes his first steps to the joy of his parents and neighbors. Child plays about the house and outside with neighboring children. Child listens wide-eyed to the bedtime stories, sometimes by Mother, sometimes by Father, every night before going to bed. Child catches a cold, is down with a fever, and is watched over by concerned parents until he gets better. Child goes to temple school, taking a kosher lunch in a pack that Mother prepares. Youth helps around in the tasks of the house, tidying up his room, setting the table, taking out the garbage. Youth learns carpentry in apprenticeship at Father's shop. Young adult now announces to parents that he is now ready to move out to seek out his own path, and Mother and Father, with mixed emotions, give him their blessing.

The main point to note in contemplating the early life of Jesus is the ordinariness of the life he led, growing up like any Jewish boy of his culture and time, living the same routine day in and day out, obeying his parents, doing his share in the household chores, experiencing all the growing pains of childhood and adolescence, gradually coming of age, learning a trade, and so on.

> Jōshū asked Nansen, "What is the Way?"
> Nansen replied, "Ordinary Mind is the Way." (*Gateless Gate*, no. 19)[15]

This Zen koan is an invitation to look at the most intimate and yet easily neglected places in which the Way manifests itself. As a seeker enters the path with an open heart, full of enthusiasm and expectation, in asking "What is the Way?" one easily imagines some grand vision of living in an exalted plane, always in an ecstatic mode and feeling deeply spiritual. This koan brings the seeker back down to earth and calls attention to the fact that the ultimate Way is right here, closer than we can imagine, right in the midst of the ordinary events of our day-to-day life. It is getting up in the morning, washing one's face, eating breakfast, going to work, walking, running, sweating, being sad, being glad, going home, getting tired, day in, day out.

I recall the blessed times I spent in the Jesuit novitiate, wherein the novice master repeatedly emphasized that the main objective—the "desired learning outcome," if you will—of this two-year period of our formation as preparation for life as a Jesuit was to enable us to directly experience the Ignatian dictum that comes from undertaking the Spiritual Exercises: "doing God's will in all things."

Our daily schedule included times for meditation and prayer, study (Latin and Greek, history of the Society of Jesus, the writings of Ignatius), spiritual reading, and also periods of work in the kitchen, garden, and other parts of the big building we all occupied, as well as periods of team play (basketball, soccer, tennis). The transition from one part of the schedule to another was signaled by a bell rung by the senior novice, and the instruction given was to drop everything one is doing upon hearing the sound of the bell and move on to the next part of the schedule.

The teaching given was as follows: if one is cleaning the utensils in the kitchen, that is God's will for you at that very moment, so put yourself into it wholeheartedly. If it is playing basketball, then play wholeheartedly. We were encouraged to embody the spirit of this teaching in the minutest details of our day-to-day life, from washing our face in the morning to preparing our beddings to go to sleep at night. This is where you will find God's will for you: right here in what you are doing. That is the Way. The Latin phrase we used to repeat in this regard was *Age quod agis* [Do what you are doing], with the implied message that in doing so, you are fulfilling God's will.

The two years I spent in the novitiate set a certain habit of mind that, while I cannot say I have maintained it all the time, somehow is there as a default mode. I learned to appreciate and cherish the ordinary tasks of day-to-day life as the place to embody the Way. Years later, after being initiated into the practice of Zen, I was able to appreciate this in a new and deeper way, with its emphasis on simply being fully present each moment in whatever one may be doing. Each moment can be the gateway to a realm that is beyond the linear flow of time from past to present to future, as it opens up and gives us a glimpse of the eternal, right *here*, *now*, in the very mundane and ordinary tasks of daily life.

Contemplating the early life of Jesus also enables us to appreciate the heart of Mary, the mother of Jesus, as she took care of him, held his hand when he was sick in bed with a fever, prodded him to do the household chores, or scolded him as a mother would sometimes need to do. She watched him gradually grow up and come of age, and throughout she "treasured all these things in her heart" (Luke 2:51). We are invited to behold all the events and encounters that come our way in our lives from day to day, with this contemplative heart that characterized Mary's entire life.

## You Are My Beloved (Matt. 3:13–17)

Then Jesus came from Galilee to John at the Jordan, to be baptized by him. John would have prevented him, saying, "I need to be baptized by you, and do you come to me?" But Jesus answered him, "Let it be so now; for it is proper for us in this way to fulfill all righteousness." Then he consented. And when Jesus had been baptized, just as he came up from the water, suddenly the heavens were opened to him and he saw the Spirit of God descending like a dove and alighting on him. And a voice from heaven said, "This is my Son, the Beloved, with whom I am well pleased."

Recall that "Spirit" is the same word as "Breath" (*ruah* in Hebrew, *pneuma* in Greek). Immersed in water and in the mystery of the Breath, a voice from the depths is heard in the stillness: "This is my Son, the Beloved, with whom I am well pleased."

I invite us to stay in that silence, to listen deeply, in the very depths of our own being, paying close attention to the breath. We may also hear the message, *You are my beloved. With you I am well pleased.*

The desire to be loved flows deeply in our hearts as human beings. Many of us spend much of our lives doing all kinds of things to fulfill what appears to be the most central of all our needs, the need to be loved. As we examine what motivates our thoughts, actions, and purposes in life, we may realize that an underlying drive remains in us seeking to please our parents or fulfill what we construe to be their expectations of us, whether they are still alive or even after they have long died. Or we may come to realize that we strive to do things in the hope that people around us will approve or think well of us. All of this activity stems from that deepest need and concomitant desire to be loved.

As we behold Jesus receiving this unconditional affirmation, our gaze turns back to our own selves, as we open the ears of our heart in the midst of the stillness. A moment may come when we hear it for ourselves: *You are my beloved; in you I am well pleased.* In the scriptural text we read this as a voice addressed to Jesus. As I breathe in and breathe out, setting my mind on the image of Jesus being baptized in the Jordan, entering the stillness of contemplative practice, a fusion of horizons may occur. In that very moment, that voice may resound through my entire being: *This is my beloved . . . in whom I am well pleased.*

As we sit quietly and allow our attention to be centered on the Breath, and as we immerse ourselves in its Mystery, our hearts may be opened to hear that same voice that addressed Jesus, and hear it also addressed to each of us as well, each in our own unique ways. This is the voice of Unconditional Love, affirming me, allowing me to be who I am as I am, filled with the confidence that I am loved just as I am, no matter what.

Experienced with intensity and impact, this moment can be a peak experience and a transformative turning point in one's life journey. This moment as such marks our entry into the Path of Union. In such a case, the remaining exercises of the Second Week, and even the Third and Fourth Weeks, will no longer be seen as an "ascent" toward the peak of a mountain but as a "descending movement" in order to have a better view of the contours of the mountain path and the terrain from the peak's vantage point.[16]

This experience of unconditional affirmation, this real-ization that *I am loved, no matter what*, is an empowering force that can propel us to live no longer seeking love, often in the wrong places, for ourselves, but in a way that gives back that unconditional love to all those around me, enough for an entire lifetime.

Led by the Breath, Jesus is empowered and ready to move on and take the next step in his path of embodying the Way.

In the midst of the Second Week devoted to contemplative exercises on events in the life of Jesus, Ignatius introduces a set of exercises meant to guide the seeker in making choices in life that come from a place of true inner freedom. We look at these exercises in the two following chapters.

## Notes

[1] I have commented on various angles of this koan in a previous work. See Ruben L. F. Habito, *Healing Breath: Zen for Christians and Buddhists in a Wounded World* (Boston: Wisdom Publications, 2006), chap. 5.

[2] I take this succinct summary of the levels of meaning of the Tao from Houston Smith, *The World's Religions* (San Francisco: HarperSanFrancisco, 1991), 196ff.

[3] See Jacob Neusner, *Judaism and the Interpretation of Scripture* (Peabody, MA: Hendrickson Publishers, 2004), and Craig A. Evans, ed., *The Interpretation of Scripture in Early Judaism and Christianity: Studies in Language and Tradition* (Sheffield, UK: Sheffield Academic Press, 2000).

[4] Wilfrid Cantwell Smith, *What Is Scripture?* (Minneapolis, MN: Augsburg, 2000).

[5] Rita Sherma and Arvind Sharma, eds., *Hermeneutics and Hindu Thought* (New York: Springer, 2008).

[6] Robert Thurman, ed., *Buddhist Hermeneutics* (Los Angeles: Kuroda Institute, 1991).

[7] R. Habito, "Bodily Reading of the Lotus Sutra," in *Readings in the Lotus Sutra*, ed. S. Teiser and J. Stone (New York: Columbia University Press, 2009), 187-208.

[8] J. K. Kadowaki, SJ, *Zen and the Bible: A Priest's Experience* (London: Routledge and Kegan Paul, 1980). I acknowledge indebtedness and here express my deep gratitude to Fr. Kadowaki, who was also my mentor while I was at Sophia University in Japan in the 1980s.

[9] See Sandra Schneiders, *The Revelatory Text: Interpreting the New Testament as Sacred Scripture*, 2nd ed. (Collegeville, MN: Liturgical Press, 1999). See also Paul Griffiths, *Religious Reading: The Place of Reading in the Practice of Religion* (New York: Oxford University Press, 1999), which highlights the import and the attitudes involved in the reading of texts with a religious message, contrasted with what the author calls "consumerist" reading.

[10] Roger Haight, SJ, *Christian Spirituality for Seekers: Reflections on the Spiritual Exercises of St. Ignatius* (Maryknoll, NY: Orbis Books, 2012), echoing Hans Georg Gadamer. "The social and cultural situation, the circumstances that influence perspective, personal background and formation, all constitute a person's standpoint and horizon of consciousness. All texts were created in a particular horizon, and they reflect it. When they are interpreted and brought to life in another context, a fusion of the two horizons occurs, the horizon of the text and the ho-

rizon of the interpreter. The fusion of narratives with specific reference to the narrative of Jesus operates analogously. It consists in drawing the story of Jesus, and all the stories that make it up, into the present situation" (85–86). I am deeply grateful to Roger for sending me an advance electronic copy of the manuscript of his book, which I was able to consult in the process of writing this one.

[11] Patrick Hart and Jonathan Montaldo, eds., *The Intimate Merton: His Life from His Journals* (San Francisco: HarperSanFrancisco, 1999), 124.

[12] Thomas Merton, *Conjectures of a Guilty Bystander* (New York: Image Books, 1968), 179–80.

[13] Used with permission of the author, treasured former colleague at the Perkins School of Theology and former president of the Iliff School of Theology.

[14] There are speculations about Jesus having joined a sect called the Essenes, where he is said to have learned much of the spiritual teachings he imparted during his public career. Various other, more imaginative accounts have Jesus going to India, Tibet, Japan, etc., learning from sages and magicians. We leave these to the level of speculation.

[15] Yamada Kōun, *The Gateless Gate* (Boston: Wisdom Publications, 2004), 92.

[16] In this case, a skilled spiritual director will offer guidance in a way that tailors the remaining sets of exercises in accordance with the needs of the individual, taking into account the particularity, the depth, and the intensity of his or her experience of this contemplative moment. We return to this point as we consider the Contemplation on Divine Love in the penultimate chapter.

# 7

# The Quality of Freedom

*Grounding Our Choices*

In a collection of Zen koans called the *Blue Cliff Records*, some cases address the question of making choices. Here is one:

> A monk asked Jōshū, "'The supreme Way is not difficult, it simply dislikes choosing.' What is non-choosing?" Jōshū said, "Above the heavens and under the heavens I am the only one, alone and exalted." The monk said, "That is still choosing." Jōshū said, "You stupid bumpkin, where is the choosing?" The monk remained silent. (*Blue Cliff Records*, case no. 57)[1]

Here the monk is quoting a verse from a poem composed by Master Sōsan, third Zen ancestor in China after Bodhidharma (d. 606).[2] A longer version is as follows: "The supreme Way is not difficult, it simply dislikes choosing. Only if there is no love or hatred, there is complete clarity."

From this passage it appears that the Zen path is averse to making choices, as this would go against "the supreme Way" (also translated as "the peerless Way"). "The supreme Way is not difficult, it simply dislikes choosing." Right there an astute reader may see the inherent contradiction in this statement: "It simply dislikes choosing" is already expressing a choice, and the saying thereby contradicts itself!

Another koan beginning with the same poem has a monk pointing out this contradiction to the Zen master.

A monk asked Jōshū, "'The supreme way is not difficult, it simply dislikes choosing.' But even if a word is uttered, it is already an action of 'choosing.'—Then how can you, Master, try to lead other people?"

The monk is raising an objection: "With self-contradictory statements like that, how can you presume to lead people to the Way?" However, anyone familiar with Zen literature cannot help but acknowledge that Zen does not shy away from contradiction, but rather seems to glory in it and even flaunt it. The second part of the koan reads as follows.

Jōshū said, "Why don't you quote the sentence to the end?" The monk said, "I just had this much in my mind." Jōshū said, "It's only: 'The supreme way is not difficult; it simply dislikes choosing.'" (*Blue Cliff Records*, case no. 59)

Rather than giving the monk a rational answer that would untangle the contradiction and help him through it, the Zen master only affirms the contradictory statement all the more boldly.

Let us look at this from another angle. Another way to translate this poem is, "The supreme Way is not difficult, it simply avoids preferences." The poem is basically affirming a long-held teaching within Zen tradition that the discriminating mind—that faculty in us that makes distinctions between "what I like" (= love) and "what I don't like" (= hate)—is not to be relied upon in matters of the Way.

Understood in this manner, we can see the resonance of this teaching with what Ignatius emphasizes at the beginning of the Exercises, right at the Principle and Foundation:

> For this it is necessary to make ourselves indifferent to all created things in all that is allowed to the choice of our free will and is not prohibited; so that, on our part, we want not health rather than sickness, riches rather than poverty, honor rather than dishonor, long rather than short life, and so in all the rest, desiring and choosing only what is most conducive for us to the purpose for which we are created. (Mullan, 19)

Another image comes up as a way of clarifying the point of the poem. Among the martial arts that came under Zen influence during the course of its development in Japanese history is the Way of the Sword, or *kendō*.[3] In a match between seasoned *kendō* practitioners, one can see how the protagonists pace across the floor very slowly with swords upraised and ready to thrust forth, each one paying full attention to every move of the other. This slowly moving, face-to-face encounter of two (wooden) sword protagonists each in full attentiveness to every minute movement or gesture of the other builds up tension in a kendō match that can grip the entire crowd of spectators with a high degree of intensity, somewhat like the tension that builds up in the last few minutes of a basketball game with both teams seesawing for the lead, driving the spectators wild with excitement. One difference is that the excitement in a kendō match is largely subdued and is not given boisterous expression as at a basketball game.

In such a situation, the kendo⁻ artist is fully attentive each moment, and if one allows a discriminating thought such as,

"What shall I do now?" or "Should I make a thrust yet?" or, worse, some other thought irrelevant to the moment, the other is immediately able to perceive that, and *whack!* The match is over. In short, the crucial "decisions" in a kendō match are not made with discriminating thought but rather with intuitive moves that come right from the core of one's awareness as fully attentive each moment. These moves are spontaneous responses to each move or gesture of the opponent as one perceives them in that state of full attention. The supreme Way is not about discerning whether to go in this direction or that but about allowing the inner voice to make the move with one's entire being that manifests itself in a very palpable and bodily manner. To make such adept moves in the Way of the Sword, emerging directly from the core of one's being in a spontaneous response to a situation, takes years and years of training. To embody the spirit of the poem, "The supreme Way is not difficult, it only dislikes choosing," in one's daily life likewise takes years of sustained Zen meditation practice.

In practical terms, how then is a Zen practitioner to deal with situations where one is at a fork in the road in one's journey in life, and a spontaneous response like the kind one could make in a kendō match is not readily available? In short, in situations in which an intuitive, right-brain-based response is not immediately evident, how may we make use of our analytic, discursive, left side of the brain to help us weigh the options carefully and clearly? Here we may turn to Ignatius for guidance. This chapter and the next examine the Ignatian approach to making choices, looking at meditative exercises presented in the Second Week.

## Two Standards

This meditation places before us two divergent paths, and we are called to make a clear-cut choice of one or the other. We are presented with an imagery of two standards or banners that represent their respective sets of fundamental values and ways of life: the standard of Satan and the standard of Christ.

This exercise is preceded by an earlier one placed at the very opening of the Second Week, a meditation on the kingdom of Christ. In this exercise, very much seeped in Ignatius's own personal temperament and cultural milieu, and in an unreflectively male-dominant tone, we are asked to imagine a magnanimous and good-hearted king calling upon those who would join him in battle to conquer territories under enemy control. To sign up and join such a king in this project would require equal magnanimity and good-heartedness on the part of those who follow his heed.

We are then invited to transpose this image of such a king to that of Jesus Christ, the King who seeks to conquer the hearts of all people and bring them into the divine reign, not by military battle, but through spiritual endeavor. One can see how such an exercise came right from the heart of and spoke directly to the soldier Ignatius, and putatively to many males of similar disposition who have undertaken the Exercises over the last four centuries. We can safely say, however, that this kind of imagery no longer appeals to most people in our twenty-first-century global culture. There have been attempts at substituting this imagery with other types, with varying degrees of effectiveness. We are not taking up this exercise here but simply noting that Ignatius places it at the opening of the Second Week as an exhortation to clarify where one's loyalties lie in this life.

The meditation on the Two Standards builds on what is already in place with the transition from First to the Second Week. At this point, seekers have resolved to turn their life around, departing from a life of self-centeredness and sin, and opening their heart and being to following the Way as

Jesus embodied it in his own life. The contemplative exercises focusing on various aspects of the life and words of Jesus that consist of the bulk of the Second Week are undertaken against this backdrop. These exercises are meant to illuminate and bring home to us particular aspects of the Way as they apply in our own lives.

Seen in this context, the meditation on the Two Standards is meant to undergird the seeker's decision to follow the Way of Jesus the Christ. We can take the banner of Christ as the symbol of everything that is life-giving, creative, wholesome, and laudable. It serves to highlight the fundamental set of values underlying the way of life of one who makes such a choice, in contrast to opposing values and ideals. The meditation confronts us with the choice of either taking the side of those things that Jesus stood for or the side of those things that may have the semblance of the good but that are found to be associated with "the enemy of our human nature."[4]

This meditation can be undertaken in tandem with the contemplative exercise on the temptations of Jesus, which we look at more closely in chapter 8. There, Jesus confronts the tempter, who entices him with wealth, fame, and power as things that could easily fall within his grasp if he so willed. Jesus rejects these in turn and instead places his total trust in the divine will, attuning himself to and heeding the promptings of the Breath in his life.

What temptations come upon us as we embark upon the Way that Jesus laid out? Let's first look at what we human beings would ordinarily seek as we go through life. A helpful framework is found in the human "wants" as laid out in the Hindu tradition.[5]

From birth and throughout the course of our lives, we naturally desire what is pleasurable and shun what is not—whatever is unpleasant or painful. These desires include different levels of whatever is pleasurable, including the pleasures of the palate and of the other senses, as well as the higher pleasures that come with the pursuit of beauty or spiritual values. The Hindu tradition affirms the pursuit of pleasure as a legitimate one and has even come up with a text offering guidelines on the optimal pursuit of pleasure—in this case, sexual pleasure, in the widely perused *Kāma Sutra* (especially the illustrated version). But the wisdom of the Hindu tradition also cautions us that the one-sided pursuit of pleasure leads to monotony, boredom, and eventually dissatisfaction. In the midst of this pursuit, we may sometimes hear a voice tugging at us from within: *Is that all there is?*

Another level of endeavor to which human beings devote time and energy is the pursuit of material wealth and possessions, and with these comes the pursuit of power. These pursuits are inevitable, as we need to provide for our basic needs of food, shelter, clothing, and the means to carry out our purposes in life. The Hindu tradition also has come up with hallowed texts that give instructions on the pursuit of power and possessions, specifically in the *Arthaśāstra* [Treatise on Pursuing Power and Possession].[6] While affirming this pursuit, we are also cautioned about its volatility and susceptibility to being thwarted. Possessions could be subject to theft or plunder. People who find themselves at the peak of political power and authority could be toppled from those positions, through intrigues by those jealous of them or by military force. Thus, individuals who engage in the single-minded pursuit of possessions and power are inevitably hounded by the anxiety and fear that whatever they may have gained in this pursuit could be taken away from them in some way or other.

A third kind of pursuit upheld in the Hindu tradition is that of duty (dharma). This pursuit originally pertained mainly to the fulfillment of what one's state of life demands, based on a highly structured social system where different roles and functions were assigned to the different social classes. To present a summarized and idealized picture of those "duties," people in the priestly class were consigned to performing and presiding over the ritualistic actions that held the community together in a common worldview. Warriors were supposed to defend the populace against outside enemies and also to maintain order within society through military might. Merchants carried out commercial activities and were charged with distributing the goods needed to sustain people's lives. The working class toiled in the fields and also labored in different services needed in running society. Further, a husband would have appropriate duties to the wife, and vice versa, as well as parents to children, friend to friend, and so on. Duties were expected patterns of behavior that maintained the social fabric. The pursuit and fulfillment of duty could thus be regarded as bringing a deeper kind of reward—a sense of satisfaction in doing what is right.

The kinds of pursuits summarized so far are not evil or dishonorable as such; they constitute legitimate and even laudable human activities. But the Hindu tradition sets these in proper light, acknowledging another kind of pursuit that trumps them all. In short, the pursuits of pleasure, power, possessions, and duty are seen as finite pursuits that yield their concomitant finite results. As such, they are not able to give human beings ultimate and lasting satisfaction. Pleasure, possessions, and power are impermanent. The pursuit of duty may bolster one's sense of belonging to something bigger than oneself, but it remains a restricted kind of satisfaction without addressing the deeper longings of the human spirit. These deeper yearnings begin to manifest as we ask questions such as, "What is the meaning of all this?"

"Who am I, really?" and "How may I live this life to the full, knowing that I will someday die?"

The Hindu tradition names this deeper kind of yearning as liberation (*moksa*) from our finitude—a pursuit of nothing less than that which is Infinite. This tradition concurs with what Augustine realized in his own life experience when he wrote, "Our hearts are restless until they rest in You" (*Confessions* I: 1-2). The Hindu tradition offers different paths with respective prescriptions toward the pursuit of the infinite. What these paths appear to share in common is an emphasis on the single-mindedness entailed in the pursuit of liberation, in a way that overshadows other pursuits of pleasure, power, possessions, and duty. In short, the pursuit of liberation calls for a radical choice, clearly setting one's priorities in life.

The meditation on the Two Standards, seen in its proper light, places us at the crossroad in our spiritual path. With all due respect, contrary to what some commentators on the Spiritual Exercises have written, I venture to say that it is no longer about a choice between good and evil, or salvation and sin, as a surface reading may readily suggest. A person who has come this far in the Exercises has already made the choice to shun evil and selfish pursuits and instead seek to follow the Way of freedom and unselfishness, as exemplified and embodied in the life of Jesus. Rather, in this case, the standard of Satan is not so much about what is blatantly evil and destructive but about what may also have the semblance of the good and laudable but that easily misleads a seeker, ultimately militating against the true Way.

The standard of Christ is meant to represent the true Way in this exercise. We are able to see the implications of this true Way in better relief in the light of the following two meditations: Three Types of Persons and Three Degrees of Engagement.

## Three Types of Persons

In this exercise we are invited to consider three kinds of persons who, by happenstance, receive a considerable amount of money; now they must figure out what to do with it. In today's terms, we could imagine an amount like a million dollars that falls into our hands.

The three persons in question seek to find inner peace and live a spiritual path—the underlying presupposition that makes this exercise relevant at all and significant for the spiritual life. We are not talking about someone who has not yet arrived at such a resolve of seeking to live a spiritual path in the light of our human ultimate destiny. A person for whom pleasure, possessions, and power are still unquestioned attractions will find this situation of coming upon a huge amount of money to be a no-brainer. Go for it! But the same reaction would not hold for someone who is earnest in the spiritual path, whose heart is no longer easily captivated by pleasure, power, and possessions, but is in search of something much more satisfying.

This root of this exercise is to find a way to handle the windfall that is in accord with the spiritual path. The different ways these three individuals address the issue provide a mirror that can shed light on our own disposition, offering a checkpoint on the quality of our inner freedom. The underlying question here is, "Am I such a person in the way I go about my day-to-day tasks and even in some important decisions I need to make in my life?"

The first kind of person, while knowing deep within that one has to make a choice and do something about the money received, remains in a state of indecision. We are presented with a psychological picture of a phenomenon that catches even the best of us in some form or other: procrastination.

Ignatius presents this phenomenon to us in an extreme form, wherein the person is not able to make any kind of decision on the matter even "until the hour of death."

The second kind of person offers a little more complicated psychological picture. This person maneuvers the situation in a way that, while keeping all the good intentions of living a spiritual life, already has decided deep within to keep the money. Such a person will find all manners of rationalization to justify keeping the money while maintaining one's lofty intentions. In other words, rather than seeking to do as God wills, persons of this class imagine God to do as they will. "God is on our side," exclaim those who have already decided that what they are doing is good for everyone else.

The third kind of person manifests true inner freedom and detachment, willing to either dispose of the money or keep it solely in accordance with what is in the best spiritual interests, that is, according to the Way one has chosen to follow. In Ignatian terms, this decision represents the true freedom of following the divine will above all and in all things in this life. The question that comes up is how to truly discern the divine will, not only in this case, but also in the different situations that we face daily. Ignatius also has a set of prescriptions in response to this question, which he lays out in his Rules for Discernment of Spirits (addressed in the next chapter).

### Three Degrees of Engagement

Another exercise that tests and challenges the quality of my freedom in the spiritual path is what Ignatius calls "three degrees of humility." "Humility" in contemporary English usage is no longer what it meant in Ignatius's context; the intent is conveyed better in rendering this term as "degrees of engagement."

The first degree or level of engagement a person can

make in matters of the spiritual life is to uphold the bare minimum: "doing good and avoiding evil," and observing all that is entailed in being a "decent human being." Such individuals are indeed worthy of praise. We wish everyone in the world were like that. People who consider themselves spiritual seekers would at least be able to identify with this level of engagement.

A second degree of engagement goes further than just the bare decency of following all the rules. This mode of engagement entails the state of mind of a person who has placed a premium on the spiritual life and has advanced to the point of "I neither desire nor am I inclined to have riches rather than poverty, to seek honor rather than dishonor, to desire a long life rather than a short life, provided that each of these alternatives equally furthers the spiritual path and conforms to the divine will for me." This degree of engagement resonates with the state of mind sought in the Principle and Foundation: an attitude of indifference to all things, as it pertains to our ultimate destiny as human beings: not to "prefer health to sickness, riches to poverty, honor to dishonor, long life to short life," but rather, "Our one desire and choice should be what is more conducive to the end for which we are created."[7]

If one considers the above more than just laudable but also admirable and heroic, albeit somewhat stoic, a third degree of engagement is presented to us as a challenge. This level can be considered as going the extra mile, or perhaps even two miles. It presupposes that the first and second degrees of engagement described above are already in place and goes still further: "I desire and choose poverty with Christ poor, rather than riches; insults with Christ loaded with them, rather than honors; I desire to be accounted as worthless and a fool for Christ, rather than to be esteemed as wise and prudent in this world."[8]

These three exercises challenge us to plumb the depth of our resolve in following the spiritual path and allow us to check the quality of our freedom in doing so. At the center of these exercises is the figure of Jesus the Christ, whom we are invited to behold, contemplate, and emulate as the embodiment of the Way that we seek.

The rest of the Second Week is thus devoted to deepening this familiarity with the heart and mind of Jesus, "that I may know you more clearly, love you more dearly, and follow you more closely."[9] But before continuing in that direction, we'll look in the next chapter at further Ignatian guidelines for making particular choices.

### Notes

[1]See Katsuki Sekida, *Two Zen Classics: Mumonkan and Hekigan-roku*, ed. and intro. A. V. Grimstone (New York: Weatherhill, 1977), 149–51, 306–11. For reference, here are other koans that begin with the same dictum:

> Jōshū, instructing the assembly, said, "'The supreme Way is not difficult; it simply dislikes choosing.' But even if a word is uttered, it is already an action of 'choosing' or of adhering to 'clarity.' This old monk doesn't dwell in clarity. Do you monks want to keep a firm hold on it or not?"
>
> At that time a monk asked, "You say you do not dwell in clarity. If so, what is there to keep a firm hold on?" Jōshū said, "I don't know, either." The monk said, "If you, Master, don't know, why do you say that you don't dwell in clarity?" Jōshū said, "You have already asked amply. Bow and withdraw." (*Blue Cliff Records*, case no. 2)

* * *

> A monk asked Jōshū, "'The supreme Way is not difficult; it simply dislikes choosing.' Isn't that the pitfall of the people of our time?" Jōshū said, "Once someone asked me like that. I am sorry that even after five years I still can't give an answer to it." (*Blue Cliff Records*, case no. 58)

* * *

> A monk asked Jōshū, "'The supreme way is not difficult, it simply dislikes choosing.' But even if a word is uttered, it is already an

action of 'choosing.'—Then how can you, Master, try to lead other people?" Jōshū said, "Why don't you quote the sentence to the end?" The monk said, "I just had this much in my mind." Jōshū said, "It's only: 'The supreme way is not difficult; it simply dislikes choosing.'" (*Blue Cliff Records*, case no. 59)

²This poem is found in the *Shinjinmei* [Faith in Mind], said to be a seventh-century composition.

³See John Stevens, *The Sword of No-Sword: Life of Master Warrior Tesshu*, repr. ed. (Boston: Shambhala Publications, 2001).

⁴Ignatius uses these words to refer to Satan, the tempter.

⁵For a succinct summary, see Huston Smith, *The World's Religions* (San Francisco: HarperSanFrancisco, 1991), 12-81.

⁶This text is likened to Machiavelli's *The Prince* for its way of giving guidelines for gaining influence in society and pursuing and maintaining political power.

⁷Louis J. Puhl, SJ, *The Spiritual Exercises of St. Ignatius, Based on Studies of the Language of the Autograph* (Chicago: Loyola University Press, 1951), 69.

⁸Ibid., 12.

⁹From a prayer of Richard, bishop of Chichester (thirteenth century), adapted into the lyrics for a contemporary musical, *Godspell*. This prayer also sums up the aspiration Ignatius offers for the Second, Third, and Fourth Weeks of the Exercises.

# 8

# Discerning My Way

## *What Should I Do?*

In our journey of life there are times when we stand at a crossroads, called upon to make a decision on whether to go one way or the other. A successful corporate executive in his or her mid-fifties begins to question, "What's it all about?" and wants to slow down and have more time to consider the big issues in life before it's too late. But to quit one's job now would mean loss of income and entail a radical change in lifestyle for oneself and one's family. A college student must decide whether to spend junior year in a study-abroad program or remain on campus to take courses that would bolster the chances of getting into graduate school. A married couple, each of whom works in different fields, finds out that they are expecting twins and are in agreement that it is important for their family life to raise children with a stay-at-home parent. What to do?

Facing a decision in life becomes an impetus for us to step back and to take time to consider our options and their implications.

Is there a Zen way of decision making? In the last chapter, we looked at a Zen poem that states, "The supreme Way is not difficult, it only dislikes choosing." As we have seen, this poem is an invitation to let go of our discriminating mind and let choices come in a spontaneous way. The Zen way of decision making, then—if such a term is appropriate—is to sit still, listen in the silence, and touch base with the depths of your being. Allow the matter to be seen in clarity from those depths, and clarity will come and guide your decision.

A verse from the *Dao De Jing* is relevant in this regard: "Do you have the patience to wait till your mud settles and the water is clear? Can you remain unmoving till the right action arises by itself? The Master doesn't seek fulfillment. Not seeking, not expecting, she is present, and can welcome all things."[1]

Sitting in stillness is an excellent way to enable us to connect with the core of our being and see our life in perspective from the point of view of this spiritual center. From there, any decision taken can be made on solid ground. Allowing ourselves simply to sit in stillness can bring clarity to the matter at hand and make the decision a clear and undoubted one. Such clarity can occur without getting into a discursive process wherein we weigh the pros and cons and determine rationally which course is more to our advantage.

In the words of a Zen master, "Sitting down, calming the mind and letting things settle out, we allow the situation to be. We live with our question and let the answers come by themselves without forcing the issue. Then, when we move, it's from a settled, calm place, and our movements will be steady and true."[2] Indeed, seeing things with a quiet mind does enable one to decide and act on things with equanimity and clarity, with humility and a heart of compassion.[3]

In contrast to what one can call a right-brained Zen approach of calming the discriminating mind and simply allowing the matter to be clarified from the experience of stillness, Ignatius prescribes a left-brained approach that makes full use of the discursive intellect and goes into a detailed examination of the pros and cons in a meticulously methodical analytic process. This exercise of the analytic faculties in discerning what is to be done in specific situations is recommended in the context of meditative and contemplative exercises that allow us to connect with our spiritual center. We are invited to pay attention to the various movements within, which Ignatius refers to as "consolations" and "desolations," and make decisions based on our reading of those movements. Thus, a sound decision can be made "when sufficient clarity and understanding is received through experience of consolations and desolations, and through experience of discernment of different spirits."[4]

Let's take a look at what Ignatius offers in terms of guidelines for arriving at or making decisions.[5] The Second Week of the Exercises includes a section titled, "Introduction to Making a Choice of a Way of Life." Ignatius first emphasizes that every choice should be made in the light of our ultimate destiny, as clarified in the Principle and Foundation at the start of the Exercises.[6]

In our early Jesuit training I recall being advised to set each decision and action in the light of the question, "*Quid ad aeternitatem?*" [How does this figure in the light of my eternal destiny?]. This approach may have originally been taken as a way of emphasizing the importance of life in the hereafter as compared with the paltriness of earthly pursuits. But from another angle, seeing our decisions and actions in the light of a horizon of the Eternal—namely that each event that happens and each act that we engage in is a precious, irreplaceable, and unrepeatable event or act of *moment*-ous import that can define our life—enables us to decide things in a way that is not based on momentary impulses or externally driven factors but rather on what our inner voice dictates and with full internal freedom.[7]

In Zen terms, every particular thought, word, and action

is seen against the horizon of an Eternal Now. This timeless horizon sheds light on every particular thought, word, or action in our day-to-day life and gives it ultimate significance. *Ordinary mind is the Way*—well and good. But how can this timeless horizon instruct us and provide concrete guidelines about making particular choices between alternatives set before us as we live our lives in time and within a given historical setting? Ordinary mind is the Way, but in proceeding should I go eastward, westward, northward, or southward with my ordinary mind, when these all seem to be feasible choices I can make, each with their own particular implications for how the rest of my life unfolds?

Here Ignatius's guidelines invoking our analytic faculties may be of help. In a segment titled, "Three Times in Which a Sound and Good Choice May Be Made," Ignatius first notes that, on some occasions, something momentous happens in our life that thereby sets the path for us in a definitive way. A flutist auditions for a major orchestra in a big city and is offered the position. An artist is commissioned to do a mural of one's own design for a big hall in a mall to be constructed. A physician tells a young married couple that they are expecting a baby, and they are thrilled at the prospect. In these examples, an inner decision coincides with the external conditions and circumstances, leaving no doubt on how to proceed.[8]

I was toward the end of my first year at the university in the Philippines when I happened to tag along on a car ride with some friends to see the coastline of Manila, about an hour away from campus. On the way back we decided to drop in at a Jesuit house to visit a priest whom one of our friends knew. While the others were visiting with the priest, I found myself ushered into the office of another priest, Fr. Benigno Mayo, SJ, who was the coordinator of vocations. Our conversation turned to what being a Jesuit entailed, beginning with entry into an initial two-year probation period called a "novitiate," followed by studies in humanities and philosophy, then an internship that involved teaching at one of the Jesuit-run schools, and then theological studies in preparation for priestly ordination, capped by another year of spiritual formation, before being "sent off" to the field for one's particular assignment as a fully formed Jesuit priest. That could be either going off to teach at a Jesuit school or university, preparing to do so with further graduate studies in a specialized field, guiding retreats using the format of the Ignatian Spiritual Exercises, or helping out in a parish in those areas where Jesuits were assigned on mission. He noted that Jesuit formation from novitiate to ordination involved a long process that took from twelve to fifteen years depending on individual capacities and specific needs, and he emphasized that no one was admitted into this process who did not have the "grace of vocation," with a wholehearted resolve to stick it out and go the long haul.

I have to confess first that it was a time when I was beginning to lose the fervor I initially had for my studies in physics. Along with twenty other students chosen nationwide, I was admitted to the University of the Philippines with a full four-year scholarship with a stipend, with advanced studies abroad as a likely prospect upon graduation. We were imbued with the lofty goal of spearheading our country's future scientific advancement. It was toward the end of the first year of studies, and I was just barely able to eke out the grades needed to maintain the scholarship—mainly because, rather than doing my math homework to a point of satisfaction, I had been spending many hours in the library poring over books in philosophy and religion, wrestling with the big questions—questions of meaning and the existence of God. I found myself absorbed in reading works of Spinoza and Pascal, and then Camus and Sartre, but also Maritain and Gilson and others. I found stimulating company with fellow students who were discussing such themes on a regular basis when we would get together for fun events at the Student Catholic Action center on the university campus. That was also where I hung out most of the time outside of class, finding congenial company among young men and women pursuing different courses of studies but who formed a bond in singing and laughing and eating together. The three who were with me in the car ride that day were also from this group.

As I was listening to Fr. Mayo describe the process of Jesuit studies and spiritual formation and what they entailed, for some reason I felt a welling up of something exciting within me, telling me, *That's what I want!* And as he was concluding his description, I surprised myself by saying to him, "Father, please give an application form." Upon completing the form I was immediately given an appointment for a requisite series of interviews to check on eligibility for admission. Three months later I entered the Jesuit novitiate with eight other young men, beginning a new adventure in my life journey.

This longwinded explanation is offered to simply provide one example of the first of Ignatius's "three times in which a sound and good decision may be made," whereby an internal disposition meets with the external conditions, and the matter is decided without further ado. We can only ascribe this to pure grace at work, and simply accept and be grateful.

Another kind of occasion for making a sound decision is when the matter is not so clear-cut, and factors on both sides of the choice pull us one way or the other. In this case, we are advised to pay attention to the inner movements of "consolation and desolation" that we can discern as we turn our gaze inward. "Consolation" refers to a feeling of inner peace, harmony, contentment, and joy, accompanied by a general sense of well-being. It may also come with a feeling of uplifting and exhilaration, yet grounded in a deep sense of tranquility. "Desolation" refers to a sense of listlessness, anxiety, and disharmony, a feeling of being low even to a point of depression. How do we make a decision in paying attention to these movements? This is where Ignatius provides detailed guidelines in his Rules for Discernment of Spirits.

There are two sets of such rules, the first for those beginning in their spiritual journey and the second for the more advanced.[9] Movements of consolation and desolation are to be read in accordance with the particular situation of the individual who experiences them. Ignatius explains these movements in the context of a worldview that took for granted the existence of good spirits and bad spirits, the latter being called "the enemy of our human nature." A given experience of consolation or desolation may be attributed to the former or the latter, depending on an individual's stage in his or her spiritual journey and on its overall effect on one's ability to make a sound decision in accordance with divine will.

For example, in those individuals who have yet to be awakened to the spiritual dimension in their lives, who are still living on a level driven by selfish wants and ambitions, Ignatius notes that the function of the good spirit is to disturb them and to rouse them from their slumbers, with stings of conscience and inner jolts that may lead them to question their self-oriented values and way of life. For such individuals, the bad spirits tend to give the sense that all is well and that there is no reason for concern. But for those who have begun their spiritual search and are earnestly seeking the way, the opposite is the case: the good spirit reinforces the direction of going further and deeper in the search, with consolations and inner assurances, whereas the bad spirit would tend to discourage, hamper, and sidetrack one's noble intentions and desires.

A helpful general guideline that Ignatius provides is to never make a decision either while in a state of consolation or desolation, but only when in a state of inner tranquility and clarity. From a state of transparency and tranquility, as we are faced with alternatives that could determine the course of our journey, Ignatius recommends further steps in what he lists as the third of the occasions for making a sound decision.

"Not being moved one way or the other" (by consolation or desolation), and thus in a tranquil state of mind, we are urged to list the advantages and disadvantages of one option and then the other. Examining these, from a state of equilibrium, we then make a choice, accompanied by a prayer that our choice be a sound one. To help in making a choice, Ignatius suggests three further steps, mentioned briefly earlier but worth revisiting here.

One is to imagine a person unknown to you but in whom you find rapport and sympathy. If such a person were to ask your advice on how to make a decision in this case, how would you advise that person? Another step is to imagine yourself at the point of death; from that vantage point, look at this moment in your life—about to make a decision on this particular case—and be guided accordingly. A third step that Ignatius suggests is to imagine yourself before the Last Judgment, wherein one's eternal destiny is to be determined. To a twenty-first-century reader, however, this last step may seem threatening and oppressive, inciting fear more than a sense of freedom.

Adapting Ignatius's guidelines, I would like to offer three general criteria that may be useful for those faced with decisions in life, three kinds of checkpoints for considering various options.

The first checkpoint relates to *inner peace*. For example, imagining myself making a particular choice among different alternatives, which one of these gives me a deeper sense of inner peace, assuring me that I can live with this choice and also that I can die in peace having made this choice? On the contrary, is the prospect of making this choice accompanied by a sense of anxiety and being ill at ease? Is something pulling me back from fully committing myself in this direction? If so, I should listen to that inner voice and not plunge headlong into that direction, but rather I should look again for the direction wherein one finds interior peace and tranquility.

A second checkpoint is *humility*. Does this option enable me to be aware of my own weaknesses and limitations, thereby acknowledging that I need to learn more and to continue to need help from others? If so, this is a sign in the right direction. On the contrary, in taking this direction or choosing a particular option, am I filled with a sense of confidence in my own strengths and talents, even with a sense of pride in my own achievements as well as my own potential that I will no doubt succeed in this? If so, step back, look at the issue again, and try to find the source of this attitude.

A third checkpoint is *compassion*. Does this option enable me to open myself more in compassion to others, and make me a more loving, caring, and responsible person to my neighbor, as well as to myself? If so, this option is faced in the right direction. On the contrary, does a certain option tend to make me more self-enclosed and contained, and less able to live in compassionate relationships with those around me? If so, then this direction is to be reexamined and avoided.

I have found these three checkpoints for a right decision most helpful in guiding individuals who come to me for advice when facing a decision in life.

James Martin, SJ, writes of an image that helped him in his own decision making:

> When I was in elementary school, our science teacher once asked our class to visit a nearby stream and draw out a glass of water, whose contents we would bring into class to peer at under a microscope. But before we could use the microscope, said our teacher, we would need to set the glass on a windowsill overnight: the water needed to clear. Plunging a glass directly into a pond will bring up all sorts of dirt, leaves, and twigs. Even after a few hours the water will still be cloudy. But if you let it settle, things become clearer.[10]

Like the water from the pond, containing all kinds of biological organisms, our everyday conscious mind is filled with things coming from our memories; from the deeper layers of our subconscious mind; from our thoughts, aspirations, inclinations, and ambitions; and so on. Allowing our mind to be still, as with the glass on a windowsill, lets the sediment and all the other elements settle, and we can see things unobstructed and with transparency.

In the invitation to stillness, Zen and the Ignatian Spiritual Exercises converge. What the latter adds is a set of helpful guidelines for our analytic (left-brain) faculties, complementing the intuitive (right-brain) faculties, to provide us with effective navigators as we course through our spiritual path.

In this convergence the figure of Jesus looms large. The central question then in discerning the way comes down to this: What would Jesus do? This is the Jesus who is the focus of the contemplative exercises of the Second Week, pointing us to our true self. This is the Jesus who is the locus of the Holy in our lives, overturning conventional wisdom and inviting us to be on the side of the little ones of the world. We find this Jesus present, alive, and guiding us from within with a gentle voice, as we sit in stillness and entrust ourselves to the Breath.

## Notes

[1] This passage is cited in a sermon "On Patience" by Zen Master Nonin Chowaney, Prairie Wind Zen Center, Omaha, Nebraska, http://www.prairiewindzen.org/patience.html.

[2] Ibid.

[3] We look at these elements later in this chapter.

[4] See Timothy Gallagher, OMV, *Discerning the Will of God: A Ignatian Guide to Christian Decision Making* (New York: Crossroad, 2009).

[5] A condensed summary of Ignatian guidelines can be found in James Martin, SJ, *The Jesuit Guide to (Almost) Everything: A Spirituality for Real Life* (New York: HarperOne, 2010), in the chapter aptly titled "What Should I Do?—The Ignatian Way of Making Decisions," 305–38.

[6] "In every good choice, as far as it depends on us, the crux of our intention ought to be simple, only looking at what we are created for, namely, the praise of God our Lord and the salvation of our soul. And so I ought to choose whatever I do, that it may help me for the end for which I am created, not ordering or bringing the end to the means, but the means to the end.

"It happens that many choose first to marry—which is a means—and secondarily to serve God our Lord in the married life—which service of God is the end. So, too, there are others who first want to have benefices, and then to serve God in them. So that those do not go straight to God, but want God to come straight to their disordered tendencies, and consequently they make a means of the end, and an end of the means. So that what they had to take first, they take last; because first we have to set as our aim the wanting to serve God,—which is the end,—and secondarily, to take a benefice, or to marry, if it is more suitable to us,—which is the means for the end. So, nothing ought to move me to take such means or to deprive myself of them, except only the service and praise of God our Lord and the eternal salvation of my soul" (translation from Anthony Mottola, *The Spiritual Exercises of St. Ignatius* [New York: Image Books, 1964], 82–83).

[7] The Ignatian term for this internal freedom in making decisions in

the light of our ultimate destiny is "indifference," that is, a state of mind of neither being predisposed to one side or the other, but totally open to what the divine will would dictate in every case.

[8]In Ignatius's words, "The first time is, when God our Lord so moves and attracts the will, that without doubting, or being able to doubt, such devout soul follows what is shown it, as St. Paul and St. Matthew did in following Christ our Lord" (Mullan, 49).

[9]See Timothy Gallagher, OMV, *The Discernment of Spirits: An Ignatian Guide for Everyday Living* (New York: Crossroad, 2005), and Gallagher, *Spiritual Consolation: An Ignatian Guide for the Greater Discernment of Spirits* (New York: Crossroad, 2007), for a very readable and detailed account of these two sets of rules.

[10]Martin, *Jesuit Guide to (Almost) Everything*, 344.

# 9

# Putting on the Mind of Jesus

*Overturning Conventional Wisdom*

Once the monks of the eastern and western Zen halls in Master Nansen's temple were quarrelling about a cat. Nansen held up the cat and said, "You monks! If one of you can say a word, I will spare the cat. If you can't say anything, I will put it to the sword." No one could answer, so Nansen finally slew it. In the evening when Jōshū returned, Nansen told him what had happened. Jōshū thereupon took off his sandals, put them on his head, and walked off. Nansen said, "If you had been there, I could have spared the cat."

Verse on the case:
Had Jōshū been there,
He would have given the command instead;
Had he snatched away the sword,
Even Nansen would have begged for his life.
(*Gateless Gate*, no. 14)[1]

The above is a well-known Zen koan from the collection compiled by the thirteenth-century monk Wu-men (Mumon in Japanese) titled, *Wumenkuan* [*Gateless Gate*]. Excellent commentaries on this collection are available in English,[2] so I do not dwell on the details of the case here, but only mention two points. In the first part of the koan, Zen Master Nansen confronts the student monks with a matter of life and death. None are able to come up with a satisfactory response, indicating that they were all still mired in their self-centered and dualistic mode of thinking and being. In the second part, Jōshū makes a response that overturns conventional wisdom and shows his inner freedom with regard to the matter of life and death, as well as his total mastery over the universe.

The verse extols Jōshū's total freedom of spirit as manifest in his way of responding to Nansen's checking question. The sword that Nansen used to kill the cat is the "sword of life and death" alluded to in many Zen sayings, the tool that the master wields to kill a Zen student's self-centered ego—the "old self" mired in a dualistic and deluded mode of being and thinking—and thus bring forth the newness of life in this total freedom of spirit.

What is the conventional wisdom that Jōshū has overturned in his unconventional response to Nansen's question—putting his sandals on his head and walking away? This is the checkpoint that each Zen practitioner is called to present in a one-to-one encounter with the Zen teacher.

If I may offer a generic answer here without revealing what happens in the one-to-one encounter, the conventional wisdom makes us think that life and death, wealth and poverty, sickness and health, honor and dishonor, success and failure, and other such pairs that are part of our experience in this life on earth are mutually opposing values, whereby one is preferred over the other. The conventional wisdom also holds that slippers are to be worn on the feet and not on the head, rich people are to be honored and poor people despised or pitied, the powerful are to be respected while the powerless are to be ignored, and so on.

As noted above, Jōshū's response to Nansen's testing question manifests his spirit of total freedom in the given situation and a mastery over life and death. Zen practice is precisely meant to cultivate and bring about this spiritual freedom and mastery in the seeker who takes on this spiritual path.

As we continue our contemplative exercises on the words and actions of Jesus, we come to appreciate how Jesus exhibited this total inner freedom and mastery over the various situations he encountered. He becomes for us no longer the son of a carpenter, an itinerant Jewish teacher who two thousand years ago walked about the land in Palestine and gathered a group of followers around him. In taking the invitation to behold Jesus in contemplative exercises, we may be able to see him as the One who shows us the Way, who points us to our true self that emerges as we die to our old self, still caught in delusion.

### The Beloved

> In those days Jesus came from Nazareth of Galilee and was baptized by John in the Jordan. And just as he was coming out of the water, he saw the heavens torn apart, and the Spirit descending like a dove on him. And a voice came from heaven, "You are my Son, the Beloved; with you I am well pleased." (Mark 1:9–10)

Ignatius recommends the repetition of certain exercises that call for further deepening and "tasting." In this spirit we again take up this passage that we looked at in an earlier chapter (based on Matt. 3:13–17). As we contemplate this pivotal moment in Jesus' life, we are given a glimpse of Jesus' identity and, more important, of our own.

We place ourselves in the setting with Jesus in the water, as we sit in stillness and pay attention to our breathing. We immerse ourselves into the waters of stillness, slowly allowing ourselves to go deeper and deeper. We remain there, rapt in the stillness. Listen. All is still. And in the midst of this, the Voice resonates throughout our entire being, *You are my beloved. With you I am well pleased.*

Jesus emerges from the water with this deep realization of what and who he was. We emerge from the stillness with this deep realization of what, and who we are. *You are my Beloved. With you I am well pleased.*

With this realization, everything else in our lives can be seen in fresh relief. The answers to life's most pressing questions somehow fall into place, as we allow that Voice to resonate within us, without us, and through everything we see, hear, smell, touch, taste, and imagine.

### In the Wilderness

And the Spirit immediately drove him out into the wilderness. He was in the wilderness forty days, tempted by Satan; and he was with the wild beasts; and the angels waited on him. (Mark 1:12–13)

As we entrust ourselves to the Breath more and more fully and become truly at home with its mysterious workings in us, we are driven out of our comfort zones, out of the conventional realities of our day-to-day life, and into "the wilderness," a place that is uncharted, unprogrammed, unknown, and dislocating from a certain point of view. But from another, more deeply rooted point of view, we would rather be nowhere else on earth, except where the Breath is there with us and where we are fully entrusted to its power. The wilderness is that which challenges and overturns our usual perceptions and patterns of behavior, enabling us to see things in a totally different light.

A Mahayana Buddhist scriptural text called the Heart Sutra[3] is used regularly for chanting in Zen practice communities; it is regarded as a succinct and clear-cut expression of the contents of the Buddha's enlightenment. The basic message of this sutra is summed up in a twofold statement: "Form is no other than Emptiness; Emptiness is no other than Form." "Form" is understood as everything that we can see, hear, smell, touch, taste, and imagine: in short, all that exists in this universe in its manifold diversity, including everything that constitutes our day-to-day life in this world of phenomena. These are the conventional realities that we are familiar with, within which we somehow find our comfort zone.

"Emptiness" subverts all that, unsettling us and cautioning us from taking the conventional wisdom as ultimate. This realm conveys to us that what we see, hear, smell, touch, taste, and imagine is not that at all. What is it then? Myriad tomes of commentary have sought to articulate "the meaning of emptiness." We do not go there at this time, but simply suggest for now that the wilderness that Jesus was driven to by the Breath, the place where he entered into deep solitude, can be read as pointing to this realm of emptiness.[4] In this solitude of the wilderness, Jesus faced the tempter.

Buddhist tradition also has it that Siddhartha Gautama, having renounced his worldly status and launched his quest for inner peace and enlightenment, was also visited by Mara the tempter on various occasions to dissuade him from his path, using all manner of wiles and argumentation to this effect. Siddhartha was told that he would be made universal monarch in seven days if he would only renounce his quest. After six years on his quest, having resolved to remain seated under the Bodhi tree to meditate in stillness until he attained enlightenment, Mara visited him.

The tempter calls forth his most beautiful daughters to seduce the Buddha-to-be. Mara also calls upon his tenfold army—consisting of lust, aversion, hunger, thirst, craving, sloth and torpor, cowardice, doubt, hypocrisy and stupidity, false glory and conceit—to attack Siddhartha and deflect him from his path. All this is to no avail. Siddhartha remains steadfast in his resolve, sitting under the Bodhi tree in stillness and attaining enlightenment. Even after becoming Buddha, he is said to have been visited by the tempter, accompanied by his three daughters, *Tanhā* (craving), *Arati* (aversion), and *Ragā* (desire). Needless to say, the Buddha is unmoved by these temptations, and he remains unwavering in the path of enlightenment, victorious over the tempter.

Jesus was no less unwavering in entrusting his entire being to the voice from within. He sees through and dispels the temptation to seek material prosperity. "One does not live by bread alone, but by every word that comes from the mouth of God" (Matt. 4:4). He is unmoved by the temptation to worldly fame, refusing to take heedless risks just to prove himself before the multitudes. "Do not put the Lord your God to the test" (Matt. 4:7). He refuses the temptation to power, seeking instead to only live according to the divine will. "Worship the Lord your God, and serve only him!" (Matt. 4:10). Having vanquished the tempter, Jesus experiences deep inner peace and receives consolation. The tempter leaves him, and angels come to wait on him (Matt. 4:11).

In this scene of the temptation, Jesus undergoes what in Ignatian terms is called a "discernment of spirits." In this process, one is faced with a decision that would affect how one conducts one's life from that point on, presented with the option of choosing two or more sets or courses of action, with the question, "Which choice is according to the will of God for me?" or "In following which option will I be able to praise, reverence, and serve God our Creator and Lord in the best way possible?" In Zen terms, which choice is the true Way? The guidelines for discernment of spirits, which we considered in the previous chapter, represent one of Ignatius's important contributions to the spiritual path.

The passage in Matthew enumerates the three temptations that Jesus faced: the acquisition of worldly wealth, fame, and power. Mark does not go into such detail, but he simply states the fact that Jesus was "tempted by Satan." In such a place of solitude, dislocated from our normal familiar surroundings and faced with uncertainty and with some amount of discomfort, our restless mind conjures images and thoughts that make us want to retrench and return to more familiar territory. As we go deeper into the stillness and begin to lose our footing, a tinge of fear can take hold of us, making us want to pull back, returning to firmer ground or to something we can hold on to for safety.

This is precisely where we are placed at a critical turning point in our journey into the depths. We are invited to trust the Breath and hold on to it for dear life, continuing the plunge into the stillness in that solitude. As we do so, letting go of our fears and proceeding deeper into the stillness with that firm trust, what happens? What awaits us is a realization of what a Latin writer noted: "In my solitude am I least alone."[5] What awaits us is an experience of communion, right in the midst of this solitude. Such communion is what Jesus experienced, bringing forth deep consolation. Here, "Angels waited on him."

This experience of the wilderness is what sheds light on Jesus' entire life—on everything Jesus says and does throughout his public career.

## The Good News

Now after John was arrested, Jesus came to Galilee, proclaiming the good news of God, and saying, "The time is fulfilled, and the kingdom of God has come near; repent, and believe in the good news." (Mark 1:14–15)

The time in which Jesus lived was tumultuous. John's arrest was a signal that the powers that be were wary of those who would undermine their authority, those who overturn conventional realities and incite people in this direction. Those in power therefore take measures to eliminate such elements. This sword would continue to hang over Jesus' head, as well as our own, as we follow the way of Jesus.

Firmly grounded in the experience of the wilderness, Jesus goes back to Galilee, his home turf, where he knows the people and the people know him. Here he proclaims the "good news of God" that is to mark his lifelong message and define who he is for the rest of human history. Jesus himself is the good news embodied.

Turning again to the Heart Sutra, the second part of the keynote statement reads, "Emptiness is no other than Form." This is also an expression of the good news. The experience of the wilderness makes itself manifest in the day-to-day realities of our ordinary life, enabling us to see and appreciate them in a totally new light. "The time is fulfilled." The time is now. A bumper sticker reads, "If not now, when?" We should ponder this message for our life and what we do with it.

"The kingdom of God is at hand." The bumper sticker continues, "If not here, where else?" The advent of the kingdom of God in our midst is the realization of our deepest and innermost longing. This is also the realization of the *kindom* of God in our midst: the realm where everyone in the entire universe of living beings recognizes one another as kin, and thereby thinks and lives accordingly.[6]

Jesus is telling us that the kingdom is right here, right now. How can this be? What manner of tidings is this? The key to understanding is in the next word.

"Repent!" In Greek, the term is *metanoeite,* a word in the imperative plural that refers to a "total transformation of mind and heart." How is this transformation to take place, and what does it entail? This again is a pivotal point that can set the course for the rest of our lives. As such, it resonates with what we have referred to earlier, as Jesus hears the voice from within: "You are my Beloved. With you I am well pleased."

A total transformation of mind and heart can take place in us as we are able to truly hear this voice addressed to us in a unique way. The realization of this unconditional Love can free us from our individual doubts, insecurities, and anxieties about our own existence. This realization grounds our place in the universe, right here at its center. This invitation, this imperative, goes in a two-way direction. "Undergo a total transformation of mind and heart, and you will realize that you are beloved, and unconditionally so, forever." Conversely, "Accept the fact that you are beloved, and you will undergo a total transformation of mind and heart." This is the good news that resonates within our entire being, calling forth upon us that the good news may be preached to the ends of the earth.

### Jesus Launches His Ministry

When the devil had finished every test, he departed from him until an opportune time. Then Jesus, filled with the power of the Spirit, returned to Galilee, and a report about him spread through all the surrounding country. He began to teach in their synagogues and was praised by everyone. When he came to Nazareth, where he had been brought up, he went to the synagogue on the sabbath day, as was his custom. He stood up to read, and the scroll of the prophet Isaiah was given to him. He unrolled the scroll and found the place where it was written: "The Spirit of the Lord is upon me, because he has anointed me to bring good news to the poor. He has sent me to proclaim release to the captives and recovery of sight to the blind, to let the oppressed go free, to proclaim the year of the Lord's favor." And he rolled up the scroll, gave it back to the attendant, and sat down. The eyes of all in the synagogue were fixed on him. Then he began to say to them, "Today this scripture has been fulfilled in your hearing." (Luke 4:13–21)

Having emerged from the wilderness "with the power of the Spirit" and with a deepened confidence, Jesus launches upon his ministry, proclaiming his message before a gathering at a synagogue. Recall that the term "Spirit" is a Latin derivative that comes from the same word as "breath." As we find ourselves plunged more deeply into the silence in the practice of sitting still, our little, self-centered "old self" is cast aside, and we become opened to the power of the Breath in us—opening up a new horizon, calling us forth with new confidence to live our day-to-day tasks grounded in this power.

Jesus reads a passage from the prophet Isaiah: "The Spirit of the Lord is upon me." This short phrase can be taken as a summation of Jesus' entire life. Recall that his birth is announced as the divine messenger, Gabriel, proclaims to Mary, "The Spirit of the Most Holy One will overshadow you." At the baptism of Jesus in the Jordan, this Spirit descends in the form of a dove and makes itself manifest, and also makes it heard, "You are my Beloved; with you I am well pleased." Jesus is led by this Spirit into the desert to immerse himself more deeply into the Mystery in solitude and silence, and he emerges after forty days and forty nights with clarity of vision and mission. This Spirit is what empowers Jesus in all he says and does throughout his ministry, as we see in many New Testament passages. At the end of his life, nailed upon the cross, Jesus utters, "Into Your hands I entrust my Spirit."

As we reflect on our own lives, we are also reminded of how each moment we live here on earth is sustained and empowered by the Breath. How is this Breath that I continue to breathe—or, better, which breathes in me and sustains me and empowers me—different from the one that brought Jesus into being, leading him to do all he did in his life and empowering him to be all that he came to be? We are invited to pay heed to this power constantly working in us, sustaining us, and empowering us, and to allow it to guide us in our lives.

As we sit with the above passage, key phrases jump out, calling for our attention.

*"Because he has anointed me"*: This term "anointed" comes with a rich background of meaning in the Jewish tradition. One level of meaning refers to the people of Israel themselves, as the ones chosen by God to manifest the divine purpose to all the nations. "Anointed" was then used to refer to the king of Israel, chosen and anointed with oil to signify the assuming of that role. As the people of Israel were dispersed in various directions by conquering nations and their leaders, they came to long for and expect a liberator sent by the Holy One who would unite them once more and return them to their ancestral land. This liberator would be identified as one who is divinely "anointed"

(*messiah* in Hebrew). At the time of Jesus, the Jewish people were under the rule of a foreign nation, the Roman Empire, a situation that gave rise to speculations and expectations that they would be saved from this oppressive condition by an Anointed One who is to come. The followers of Jesus, who came to form a cohesive community after Jesus' death, identified themselves by their proclamation that "Jesus is the Messiah," the Christ of God. This term "Christ" thus came to be a proper noun and identifier of Jesus the Christ.

*"To preach the good news to the poor"*: We find frequent references to "the poor" in the Jewish Scriptures with which Jesus himself was familiar. These references revolve around the divine injunction to care for "the poor among you"— specifically, the needy, the widowed, the orphan, and the alien in our midst. What does this good news entail?

The entire Christian tradition has been of a unified voice, if not always embodying it with a concomitant lifestyle, emphasizing a "preferential option for the poor."[7] For many of us blessed with a life that enables us to identify as "middle class," the poor are those unfortunate people who become the object of our sympathy. We might feel moved to write a check every now and then to help those people and somehow alleviate their need. Some Christians have an attitude such as, "Handouts only make the poor more dependent on others, so let them lift themselves up by their bootstraps." In any case, talk of "the poor" for many of us tends to be in the third person, about "those people out there."

But imagine a period when you yourself may fall into hard times, struggling to pay the rent or laden with an insurmountable debt that you have no idea how to pay back. You may become penniless and homeless, ill and unable to go to a hospital, or hungry and unable to buy food. Sit with this thought and let it sink in, as an actual possibility that could happen to you. At such a time, you may then be able to see the poor in a different light. As I imagine myself placed in such a situation, I open my eyes and ears, and those whom I had looked at as the object of pity or perhaps even with disdain are now no longer seen as "other" to me. I may happen to see a homeless man on a street corner, or a lady at the parking lot of the grocery store pushing a cart that contains not her groceries but her clothes and some scraps she picked up at a garbage bin. Suddenly, with a shock, I come to realize, "That's me!" When such a thing happens to us, the good news has entered our hearts, inevitably transforming the way we live our lives.

A doctor friend of mine works at a large, public-funded hospital. On a certain day, she told me, she was so busy attending to patients that she did not have time to grab a bite to eat for lunch. She continued to go about her work, and around mid-afternoon she began to feel sharp hunger pangs. She still could do nothing about it for a couple of hours more until the last patient was seen. During that period, when she was feeling those hunger pangs so intensely, she stopped for a moment as a flash of realization came to her: "This must be what all those children we read about in the papers who go to bed hungry every night all over the world feel all of the time."

At that moment, she related to me, this pang of hunger that she was feeling right there at the pit of her own stomach became the hunger of all the hungry children of the world, and she burst into tears. From that point on she was able to understand the issue of world hunger no longer as something that referred to "those poor people out there" but as a matter that was now intimately connected to her own life and being. She thereby began to take steps with her family to be more engaged with issues of hunger and poverty, as they continued to live their lives from day to day.

*"To proclaim release to the captives"*: Who are the cap-

tives? Why are they captive, or to what are they captive? What kind of release is proclaimed to them? We are invited to reflect on our own lives and ask ourselves, *What are the things I am captive to?* Perhaps I have not noticed certain things in myself, in my attitudes or in the way I lead my life, wherein I have fallen captive to something external to me. What are those things that I can include among my addictions, my habits of thinking and behaving that tend to diminish my freedom of spirit and ability to live true to myself? My liberation begins in recognizing and acknowledging these elements in my life and discerning how to go from there.

Further, as we look more deeply, we may notice how we think, say, and do things motivated by greed, ill will, and ignorance. In so doing, we cause others to suffer as well. What does release from this kind of captivity entail in my own life? The antidote to greed is generosity. The antidote to ill will is goodwill. The antidote to ignorance is the wisdom that sees things as they are. This is the good news, that it is possible to live in this way, freed from captivity. The overturning of these three poisons into their antidotes is a key for this good news to happen in our own lives.

*"Recovery of sight to the blind"*: Who are the blind? The obvious reference is to people with physical blindness, but another level of meaning to this term is evident. What are the blind not able to see? If we see things from the perspective of our little I-me-mine perspective that occupies the center of our world, we are blind to the reality of our interconnectedness with all beings and are thus not able to see that the well-being of all is key to our own well-being. Conversely, seeing that a way of life that seeks the happiness and well-being of all, rather than being caught up in a self-centered view that seeks my own well-being over and above that of others, is the key to this recovery.

*"To free those who are oppressed"*: Who are the op-

pressed? From what kinds of oppression are they in need of liberation? As I examine the socioeconomic and political structures of our society, am I able to notice how I am part of a structure of oppression that continues to make the poor poorer and the rich richer? To what degree can I acknowledge my complicity in such structures of oppression? And as I recognize and acknowledge my complicity, what steps can I take to minimize if not liberate myself from it? Reflecting further, am I not also a victim of oppression in subtle ways myself, at the same time as I am a perpetrator who is part of and beneficiary of the system? How may I learn from Jesus' freedom of spirit, and from his attitudes and way of life that overturns conventional wisdom, to help me toward realizing freedom from oppression, for myself as well as for my fellow human beings?

*"To proclaim the year of the Lord's favor"*: In Jewish culture, every fiftieth year is proclaimed as a "jubilee year," an auspicious time when debts are to be forgiven and slaves freed. Leviticus 25:10 reads, "And you shall hallow the fiftieth year and you shall proclaim liberty throughout the land to all its inhabitants. It shall be a jubilee for you: you shall return, every one of you, to your property and every one of you to your own family." In this time, divine favor abounds. When does this "year of the Lord's favor" begin? Again, let us take heed from the bumper sticker: if not now, when?

*"Today, this scripture is fulfilled in your hearing"*: This statement is the culmination of the entire passage that Luke cites from Isaiah. Today is the day when all these wonderful things take place. Right here, right now. What manner of proclamation is this? In another passage Jesus tells his listeners who are surprised and shocked at what he is saying to them, "Let anyone with ears to hear listen!" (Mark 4:23). In short, awaken to the dynamic reality of the present moment, and you will realize the good news.

We are invited to behold all this from the perspective of this Breath that breathes within me, in and out, in and out, right here, right now, each moment. Breathing in, breathing out, we open our eyes, our ears, all our senses, our heart, and our mind, and we allow this present moment to take center stage. What do you see? Right here, right now, as we allow ourselves to be fully in this present moment, wherein the entirety of the past and the open horizon of the future are collapsed into this timeless now, time stops, and we are given a glimpse of the realm wherein the poor hear the good news and are thereby rendered no longer poor. From this vantage point we are able to behold that realm whereby the captives are released, the oppressed are freed, and the blind are able to see.

In this realm, divine Love reigns, and each and every person is full and replete and welcomed just as they are—the realm of the kindom of God. From the vantage point of this realm where divine Love reigns, the real world of our own time—wherein the poor remain in their state of destitution, the captives and the oppressed cry out for freedom, and the blind cry out for light—comes into full relief, calling forth our response. This response can only one of divine Love, out of a heart of compassion. From this moment on, seeing things from this vantage point, we take on the heart and mind of Jesus, ready to devote our entire lives to make that realm that we have glimpsed into a reality. We are able to understand the mind of Jesus as he proclaims, "I came to bring fire to the earth, and how I wish it were already kindled!" (Luke 12:49).

> All spoke well of him and were amazed at the gracious words that came from his mouth. They said, "Is not this Joseph's son?" He said to them, "Doubtless you will quote to me this proverb, 'Doctor, cure yourself!'

And you will say, 'Do here also in your hometown the things that we have heard you did at Capernaum.'" And he said, "Truly I tell you, no prophet is accepted in the prophet's hometown. But the truth is, there were many widows in Israel in the time of Elijah, when the heaven was shut up three years and six months, and there was a severe famine over all the land; yet Elijah was sent to none of them except to a widow at Zarephath in Sidon. There were also many lepers in Israel in the time of the prophet Elisha, and none of them was cleansed except Naaman the Syrian." When they heard this, all in the synagogue were filled with rage. They got up, drove him out of the town, and led him to the brow of the hill on which their town was built, so that they might hurl him off the cliff. But he passed through the midst of them and went on his way. He went down to Capernaum, a city in Galilee, and was teaching them on the sabbath. (Luke 4:22–31)

People who are not able to understand what Jesus is saying here have reason to be surprised and annoyed at his words. The people who would rather keep the status quo, where the poor, the captives, and the oppressed are kept in their place (that is, out of sight and out of mind), have reason to feel threatened by Jesus' sayings. The natural reaction is to reject him, to run him out of town, to get him out of our lives. We have our riches and our vested interests to lose if we let Jesus' vision get the better of us.

We are thus confronted with a choice, which will now determine the course of the rest of our lives. Do we open our hearts, let Jesus and all that he stands for come into our lives, and live in the light of his vision and mission? Or do we hold on to our securities, choose the status quo, and join those who run Jesus out of town and out of our lives?

## The Blessed Ones

When Jesus saw the crowds, he went up the mountain; and after he sat down, his disciples came to him. Then he began to speak, and taught them, saying:

"Blessed are the poor in spirit, for theirs is the kingdom of heaven.

"Blessed are those who mourn, for they will be comforted.

"Blessed are the meek, for they will inherit the earth.

"Blessed are those who hunger and thirst for righteousness, for they will be filled.

"Blessed are the merciful, for they will be shown mercy.

"Blessed are the pure in heart, for they will see God.

"Blessed are the peacemakers, for they will be called children of God.

"Blessed are those who are persecuted for righteousness' sake, for theirs is the kingdom of heaven." (Matt. 5:1–12)

This passage, called the Sermon on the Mount, is one of the most famous texts of the New Testament, conveying the heart of Jesus' teaching. Called "the Beatitudes" (*beatus/beata* = Latin for blessed, fortunate, blissful, happy), it provides a succinct statement of the good news to all people. The Greek term is *makarios*, which has the connotation of "prosperous, fortunate." Scholars say that the term was originally used to describe the Greek divinities in the pantheon, as beings with prosperity and power. The term also came to be applied to human beings who had died and gone beyond this world's woes and cares, and were thereby "blessed" and "fortunate." Further, the term came to be applied to those people in this world who were indeed, from an economic and social perspective, prosperous and fortunate in their status in life: the elite, the rich, the high and the mighty—society's powerful ones.

This teaching of Jesus in the Gospel of Matthew conveys a message that truly overturns conventional wisdom. The ones who are truly prosperous and fortunate, the ones to be emulated, are not whom you would normally think. Consider Jesus' words:

*"Blessed are the poor in spirit, for theirs is the kingdom of heaven"*: The "poor in spirit" can mean one who is spiritually deprived or lacking in a sense of spiritual values, whether one has material possessions or not. Evidently from the context, though, this is not what this passage is about. It has also been taken as "not materially poor, but in spirit only," which means a person who could be materially rich but is not attached to those riches. This interpretation of the term appears to be the more widespread. On this point, the version of the Beatitudes found in Luke, with its outright and direct use of "the poor" (Luke 6:20: "Blessed are you who are poor, for yours is the kingdom of God"), is contrasted with Matthew's "poor in spirit," with some commentators suggesting that Matthew has watered down the message.

A Zen koan titled "Seizei the Poor" from the *Gateless Gate* may be helpful here.

A monk, Seizei, eagerly asked Master Sosan, "I am solitary and poor. I beg you, Master, help me become prosperous."

San said, "Venerable Zei!"

Zei said, "Yes, Master."

San said, "You have already drunk three cups of Hakka wine, and you still say that you have not moistened your lips." (*Gateless Gate*, no. 10)[8]

The koan is an invitation to consider and take stock of our own situation as "solitary and poor," like the monk Seizei. We, like Seizei, are tempted to turn to others who we think may have some more than ourselves and ask for assistance. "Help me become prosperous."

Master Sozan's closing statement, "You have already drunk three cups of Hakka wine, and you still say that you have not moistened your lips," is meant to call our attention to the hidden wealth that remains untapped in us. Hakka wine is said to have been the finest in China of that day, and to be able to drink it indicates one's prosperous status. Master Sozan appears to be saying, "Look and see how wealthy you are already! What is this talk about being solitary and poor?"

If we take this koan only at the surface level, we may think that we are being told the same old cliché, "Don't complain, count your blessings." But the Zen master is speaking of something much deeper than that. He is inviting us to plumb the depths of our being, to open our eyes to the wondrous treasures available therein—more than enough to last for a lifetime and beyond. Our eyes will be opened to this realm as we give ourselves the opportunity to "stop and see"—following the Buddha's invitation to be still and awaken the dynamic reality of each present moment. From this vantage point, we may be able to hear for ourselves the "good news to the poor."

A commonly taken path in reading the Beatitude passages is to understand them as referring to the eschatological, that is, the horizon of the future when the reign of God will finally become fully manifest. In such a reading, the message would seem to be, "Bear your sufferings now, for in the future (or after you die and go to heaven), your reward will be great." This explanation has been the refrain of much Christian preaching through the ages and even in our times: "Bear your troubles with dignity and patience now, and you will get your prize in the hereafter."

But we can read this passage and the following ones as well in another way. The Greek for "poor in spirit" is "*ptokoi to pneumati,*" which can also be rendered as "those who have emptied themselves of everything, entrusting all to the Breath." What about such persons? Theirs is the kingdom of heaven; they have nothing lacking here on earth and are filled to the brim.

This paradox is the one that Jesus proclaims: those who empty themselves are the ones who live in genuine fullness of life. Jesus is not talking about a future acquisition of wealth by those deprived of it in the present. This message is for the here and now. Empty yourself and find true richness.

A Zen story tells about a monk whose abbot instructed him to transport a precious golden Buddha statue from their home temple to another temple in another town. The monk took the precious statue and wrapped it in silk, placing it inside a beautiful ornate box. He used a cart pulled by a bullock to transport the box to his destination in the next town. Along the way, robbers came, beat him unconscious, and took the cart, the bullock, the box with the golden Buddha, and even the monk's clothing, leaving him lying in a ditch beside the road. When the monk regained consciousness it was already night, and a resplendent moon was shining in the sky. He looked around and realized what had happened: no cart, no bullock, no golden Buddha, and he lying there in his underclothing, still feeling the pain from the robbers' blows. He looked up at the moon in the sky, and his first statement was, "Ah, I wish I could have given this beautiful moon to those robbers as well!"

Of course this narrative is fictional, but it describes the picture of one who, having no earthly riches, having everything taken away, is still able to live with a heart full of the wealth of the universe. The story is not about the future; it is about a total transformation of heart and mind that we are invited to, here and now. This is Jesus' invitation to all of us: Repent, and receive the good news into your hearts! The same theme is repeated in the succeeding Beatitudes.

*"Blessed are those who mourn, for they will be comforted":* This statement refers to people who have lost something precious and mourn the loss. We should reflect on the things so precious to us, whose loss we would mourn. We each might come up with a different list: a person we love, our job, our social status or reputation, our material possessions, our good looks, our health. The loss of someone or something we cherish is a big blow to our sense of stability and well-being.

Most precious for many of us is not the person we love or the particular object that we cherish, but our own little I-me-mine that clings to the idea that I will be miserable and unhappy if I lose *this* beloved person, *this* particular object. When an actual tragedy happens in our lives, we mourn the change of the situation from one wherein we felt we were in control and in a good place as long as this person is with us, or as long as we have this or that in our possession, and so on. But if we let go of the idea that our happiness depends upon being with this beloved person or having this particular object in our possession, and be totally open to what the new situation beckons, we may gain an entirely new perspective.

Consider this well-known Chinese story, told and retold in different versions:

A man named Sei Weng owned a beautiful mare which was praised far and wide. One day this beautiful horse disappeared. The people of his village offered sympathy to Sei Weng for his great misfortune. Sei Weng said simply, "That's the way it is." A few days later the lost mare returned, followed by a beautiful wild stallion. The village congratulated Sei Weng for his good fortune. He said, "That's the way it is." Some time later, Sei Weng's only son, while riding the stallion, fell off and broke his leg. The village people once again expressed their sympathy at Sei Weng's misfortune. Sei Weng again said, "That's the way it is." Soon thereafter, war broke out and all the young men of the village except Sei Weng's lame son were drafted and were killed in battle. The village people were amazed at Sei Weng's good luck. His son was the only young man left alive in the village. But Sei Weng kept his same attitude: despite all the turmoil, gains, and losses, he gave the same reply, "That's the way it is."[9]

The comfort here is in letting go of the idea that happiness and well-being are conditioned by this external factor of being in the company of someone we long for and love, or continuing to have some particular object in our possession. Letting go of this idea, of a condition we impose upon ourselves to be able to find happiness, is what sets us free to welcome and cherish each situation that comes our way, just as it is, and celebrate it with a heart of gratitude.

*"Blessed are the meek, for they shall inherit the earth"*: This Beatitude echoes Psalm 37:11: "But the meek shall inherit the land, and delight themselves in abundant prosperity." Being meek appears to run against the culture of rugged individualism valued in modern Western society. In this society, this slogan from an ad for a business venture—"You get what you negotiate, not what you deserve"—would be

the guiding norm for behavior. Meekness is often construed as a passive attitude, a stance of weakness and compliance with a stronger power. Friedrich Nietzsche identified such an attitude, along with humility and kindness, with "slave morality," opposing this to "master morality" characterized by pride, strength, nobility.

The stance that this Beatitude upholds, however, is not a passive and compliant one, but rather an open-hearted, trusting, welcoming attitude that allows situations of adversity to take their course without resisting or complaining. What comes to mind is the attitude cultivated in East Asian martial arts, like judo or kendō or aikido, where one takes a stance that is far from passive, but rather alert, attentive, ready to respond to thrusts from the opponent with a parry that uses the opponent's strength and turns it around to subdue it and bring the situation back to harmony.

Such persons who are able to live with a heart that cultivates this kind of harmony, Jesus proclaims in this Beatitude, have everything they could possibly need and rest content in their hearts. As one saying goes, the truly rich are not those who have what they want but those who want what they have and live in contentment.

*"Blessed are those who hunger and thirst for righteousness, for they will be filled":* The word "righteousness" (from the Greek *dikaiosune*) refers to the trait that makes a person acceptable in divine sight, that which makes one "justified." This theme is central to the understanding of the Christian message, and has had a long history of theological discourse. The Greek contains the nuance of "the state that one ought to be," that is, a way of life and mode of being congruent with what one is right from the start, signifying one with purity of heart and mind, and a sense of justice and integrity. "Righteousness" is clearly different from "self-righteousness."

In Buddhist terms, righteousness is about a person who is at home with one's own true self. The beginning of the search for one's true self, one's Buddha nature, is called "the awakening of the Bodhi mind." To "hunger and thirst for righteousness" is the same as a state of mind that is earnest in the search of one's true self, an earnest spiritual seeker. To recognize and accept yourself as such, as a spiritual seeker, is to be assured that what you seek is already given to you.

A friend told me the true story of her travel to India in search of spiritual guidance from a master. When she finally met this well-known guru in a formal audience, he asked her, "What do you want?" Her response from the heart was, "I want to see God face to face." He responded, "You have what you want. But it will take a lot of work." Another twenty years of earnest search passed, accompanied by a sustained practice of meditation, before she began to understand and appreciate what the guru meant.

*"Blessed are the merciful, for they will be shown mercy"*: Who are the merciful? They are those whose heart is open to others, loving and compassionate, and welcoming and forgiving. This Beatitude speaks of what we can call a "benevolent cycle" (the opposite of a "vicious cycle"). People who have an experience of being given mercy are the ones who are empowered to offer mercy to others. The more one opens one's heart in mercy, the more one receives mercy from others as well.

We see this in another saying of Jesus, in Luke 6:38. "Give, and it will be given to you. A good measure, pressed down, shaken together, running over, will be put into your lap; for the measure you give will be the measure you get back." But the other angle to see here is that we are empowered to love others in the measure that we ourselves realize we are loved. As we sit in stillness and open our hearts, we are enabled to hear that voice, again and again: *You are my beloved. In you I am well pleased.* And the more we are confirmed in this hearing, the more empowered we are to live our lives in the only way we can, offered in return for this love.

*"Blessed are the pure in heart, for they will see God":* We naturally associate "pure of heart" with a child, still innocent, open-hearted, and spontaneous. Indeed, we find purity of heart in little children. Jesus himself points to the little children in teaching his listeners about the reign of God (Matt. 18:3; 19:14), and we tend to lament that we ourselves lose this purity of heart as we grow older and wiser in the ways of the world. Maybe so. But as I mentioned earlier, we all have experiences of looking at an infant held by a mother or father, or in a stroller, and the sight of the innocent face of the baby draws forth a smile in us, and a soft and tender feeling in our heart. At that moment, the purity of heart that is our own deepest self is touched and activated at the encounter with another who is pure of heart.

A basic Buddhist view is that our innate nature is to be pure of heart. But somewhere along the way, the self-centered ego, that which always sees things centered on the I-me-mine, gets in the way and brings on outside elements that cover up this innate purity. The practice of Buddhist meditation, in its different forms as they developed over time, is considered as a way of polishing away those stains and allowing one's innate purity to manifest itself again in its pristine clarity.

Sitting in stillness allows the dust and dirt that may have accumulated and which blocks our view of things as they really are—that is, as seen with a pure heart—to fall away. The practice of meditation may sometimes present a struggle, when one has an active mind that goes all over the place; attempts to keep the mind focused in the here and now are made to little avail. But the very earnestness that we put into it, as we continue in a steadfast way to give ourselves time for relishing the silence as part of our day-to-day life, bears its fruit. We may be gifted with moments of clarity, with glimpses of the way things are from a perspective of that innate purity. It may be a moment of just looking at a flower, a blade of grass, a pebble. It may be looking in the eyes of someone we love or listening to a musical piece. Or it could come to us while taking a walk around the neighborhood, feeding goldfish, stroking the neck of a horse, or patting a dog's soft fur. In such moments, time stops; the I-me-mine disappears from view, and the sky opens in all its transparent clarity. Those moments are indeed gratuitous and grace-filled, standing out as milestones in our life journey. In those moments we are gifted with a glimpse of the face of God.

*"Blessed are the peacemakers, for they will be called children of God"*: I met Fr. Michael Rodrigo, a Catholic priest of the Oblates of Mary Immaculate from Sri Lanka, at an international Buddhist-Christian conference held in Berkeley, California, in August 1987. He was a participant in some of the sessions I attended. At that time I was still in active ministry as a Jesuit priest working in Japan and was among a small circle of people who came to befriend him and enjoy his company during those few days of the conference, sharing our experiences as Christians engaging in dialogue with Buddhists. He had a double doctorate, one in theology from Rome and one in comparative religions from Paris, but he set aside a career as a university or seminary professor and served as pastor of a Catholic parish in a small village in Sri Lanka. For many years his country had seen much violence and bloodshed between the majority Sinhalese (Buddhist) and a minority Tamil (Hindu) populace. As a Catholic priest he tried to take on the role of a mediator for the opposing sides, devoting himself to peace work among the people in his local area. He also intervened frequently on behalf of young people being arrested by the military.

A few months later, we heard that Fr. Mike, as we endearingly called him, had been gunned down by assailants as he was celebrating Mass in his parish church. Fr. Michael Rodrigo continues to be remembered by his people to this day, especially by those who work for peace. In 2002 a folk monument and shrine were built in his honor near the place where he was killed, and his death continues to be commemorated as an inspiration for people on their way to a peaceable future for their country.

The circumstances of Fr. Mike's death recall those of Archbishop Oscar Romero of El Salvador, another martyr (witness) for peace. This Beatitude refers to individuals like Fr. Mike and Msgr. Romero, and so many others who lived and died for peace. The fact that we feel uplifted and inspired upon hearing or reading their stories is an indication that the seeds of the peacemaker also lie deep in our own hearts. How can acknowledging the peacemaker in our own heart unfold in the way we live our life in a world of violence and conflict?

*"Blessed are those who are persecuted because of righteousness, for theirs is the kingdom of heaven"*: Once again we encounter the term "righteousness," which, as we noted, refers simply to a state of being true to one's own nature, one who has "found favor in the eyes of God" and is thereby at peace with oneself. Why would such a person be subject to persecution?

As a freshman in college I had a friend I will call Max, with whom I spent much time in conversations into the night on the big questions, "the meaning of it all," whether the universe is a friendly place, how one can live an authentic life amid all the unknowns and in the face of the apparent absurdity of the entire enterprise, and so on. In the middle of one conversation he went off topic all of a sudden and said, "You know, I can't stand that guy Jimmy," referring to an acquaintance who had poetry published in the campus-wide student newspaper, and also known for offering his friendly smile to everyone. When I asked him why, Max's reply was, "Because he's found himself. Just look at those poems he's written." Max was earnest in his own quest for meaning and for his place in the scheme of things—he was in a state of inner turmoil—and he could not stand the sight of someone who had already been through what he was still going through, and who had apparently found answers and come to inner peace. I could see that Max was saying this in earnest, partly in exasperation and partly in jest. I could also hear this statement coming from within him in a way that reflected his own struggle to find peace.

Max's comment gives me an inkling of how those whom we deservedly call "righteous" could be irritating to others and are open to persecution from those lacking peace and righteousness in their own lives. One of Reinhold Niebuhr's well-known works is *Moral Man and Immoral Society*, which details the background whereby people who live in an authentic way with integrity and true to their own nature are bound to find themselves at loggerheads with a society dominated by selfish interests and power plays. In such a context, a "moral person" finds oneself like a fish going upstream, by virtue of just being true to oneself and taking a stance vis-à-vis the prevalent trends in society. In doing so, such a person can be the object of persecution of those who follow the herd mentality.

This Beatitude affirms that the kingdom of heaven belongs to the righteous. Here again we are not talking of some reward in the afterlife or an ulterior motive urging us to be good. Rather, Jesus' statement offers us a glimpse of a way of being that embodies the place that we all aspire to be. Arriving there is its own reward, a realization that surpasses all earthly reward.

In sum, the eightfold Beatitudes presented in Matthew's Gospel offer us a way of being that resonates with our own deepest aspirations. The Beatitudes are also consistent with what we read elsewhere in the Gospels about Jesus' mind and heart. The picture that emerges is one that would overturn the conventional wisdom of the world.

Let us turn to other passages in contemplation to fill in the picture further.

### Eternal Life

Just then a lawyer stood up to test Jesus. "Teacher," he said, "what must I do to inherit eternal life?" He said to him, "What is written in the law? What do you read there?" He answered, "You shall love the Lord your God with all your heart, and with all your soul, and with all your strength, and with all your mind; and your neighbor as yourself." And he said to him, "You have given the right answer; do this, and you will live."

But wanting to justify himself, he asked Jesus, "And who is my neighbor?" Jesus replied, "A man was going down from Jerusalem to Jericho, and fell into the hands of robbers, who stripped him, beat him, and went away, leaving him half dead. Now by chance a priest was going down that road; and when he saw him, he passed by on the other side. So likewise a Levite, when he came to the place and saw him, passed by on the other side. But a Samaritan while traveling came near him; and when he saw him, he was moved with pity. He went to him and bandaged his wounds, having poured oil and wine on them. Then he put him on his own animal, brought him to an inn, and took care of him. The next day he took out two denarii, gave them to the innkeeper, and said, 'Take care of him; and when I come back, I will repay you whatever more you spend.' Which of these three, do you think, was a neighbor to the man who fell into the hands of the robbers?" He said, "The one who showed him mercy." Jesus said to him, "Go and do likewise." (Luke 10:25–37)

This passage is preceded by an exchange between Jesus and an "expert" on the law and the prophets, on the most important question we can ask as human beings, thrown into this earthly, mortal life. What can we do, what must we do, to find liberation from our mortality, to overcome the throes of our impending death, to realize eternal life? Jesus' initial answer is totally in consonance with the understanding of his listeners, devoted followers of the Jewish tradition and adherents of the received teaching of their divinely chosen status. "What do the law and the prophets tell you?" The response was an affirmation of their shared tradition. "Love the Lord your God with your whole heart and whole soul and whole mind and whole strength, and your neighbor as yourself." But to the question, "Who is my neighbor?" Jesus' answer subverts the expectations and the entire value system of his listeners, all good observant Jews, with the story of the Samaritan.

From historical sources, speaking in general, we know that the Samaritans at the time were despised by Judeans and regarded as second-class citizens in society. Jesus offers this story as a response to the question of who truly embodies eternal life. A priest, normally esteemed as the divine representative among the people due to his religious role, and a Levite, also esteemed for his learning and for role as interpreter of the law, are both portrayed as missing the mark in this case.

They may have had their good reasons for not stopping to help the wounded stranger. The priest may have been on the way to perform his religious duties at the temple; touching someone wounded would have rendered him impure and thus incapable of doing what people were counting on him to do for them at the temple. The Levite may have had his legitimate excuse. He may have been concerned that he would arrive late for his lecture on the law that a crowd was expecting him to deliver, and to tarry with helping someone wounded would have caused the disappointment of many people waiting for him to deliver his lecture. We, too—with our busy lives and our responsibilities to family, society, and our religion—have our legitimate excuses.

The Samaritan in the story could also have had his excuse. He may have been on the way to purchase some necessities for his family, and they were expecting him to be back on time. He may have been on his way to an important meeting with some associates on some business plan they were about to launch, and so on. But all of that fell by the wayside, once he set eyes on the wounded stranger. In some translations, the text tells us, "When he saw him, he felt compassion toward him."

What is translated in English as "compassion" comes from the Greek, *splanchnizomai*, which literally means, "to be moved from one's gut" (in the first-person singular). *Splanchna* is a noun that means "upper viscera" or "gut," sometimes translated as "bowels." The verb form used in this text is translated as "feeling compassion," or literally, "being in pain with," in seeing the situation of the wounded one and feeling the pain in one's own gut. In short, at the very moment when the Samaritan saw the wounds of the stranger, he was moved right at the core of his own being and felt the pain as his own. From this vantage point, what happened next was the most natural thing for such a person to do: everything possible to assuage the pain that is one's very own.

The key to understanding the story of the Good Samaritan is thus in this one word, *splanchnizomai*, which conveys a state of mind and a constant disposition I can have vis-à-vis the world. We look at the world and other living beings around us, and we see them not as separate objects out there that we can use or not use, according to our own designs and plans for our own happiness. Rather, we see them in the light of their intrinsic connection to us, as constitutive of who we are in ourselves.

From this perspective, "to love my neighbor as myself" is to speak a redundancy, given that the fate of my neighbor is inevitably and intrinsically tied up with my own. When I am caught up in my own individual and self-oriented world, I am unable to see wherein "my neighbor" and "myself" are intimately intertwined at the core, at our *splanchna*. With the story of the Samaritan, Jesus was revealing this world to his listeners, the world wherein eternal life reigns.

Seen in this light, the oft-repeated story of the Good Samaritan is not a moralistic story that enjoins us to help our neighbor in need, so that we may merit eternal life, but is a description of where that eternal life is manifested, and how it is fully activated in our day-to-day lives.

## Summary: Jesus, the Way

There are also many other things that Jesus did; if every one of them were written down, I suppose that the world itself could not contain the books that would be written. (John 21:25)

This concluding sentence of John's Gospel conveys a sentiment in offering glimpses of various angles of the mind and heart of Jesus in the selected New Testament texts. Volumes more could be written with contemplative exercises based on various scenes in the life of Jesus as presented in the Gospels. In this chapter I selected key passages that ultimately provide at best a limited and partial—in both senses of the word—picture, offered to the reader who is seeking the Way.

"I am the way," Jesus proclaims to his followers (John 14:6).

In contemplating Jesus' mind and heart as revealed in these passages, what comes up is a deeper understanding and appreciation of Jesus as a human being fully alive, fully present in his everyday encounters. In contemplating his words and actions, we can see clearly how his responses to situations overturn conventional wisdom, coming as they do from a deeply rooted inner freedom grounded in unconditional love.

This love is both the Love he himself receives from an unconditional Source, which he heard proclaimed by that voice he heard on the Jordan—"You are my Beloved; with You I am well pleased"—as well as the unconditional love he freely offers to all those who come to him, even those he castigates for their hardness of heart. This contemplative practice centered on Jesus can shed light on how we ourselves are called to embody the Way in our own lives.

### Notes

[1] Yamada Kōun, *The Gateless Gate: The Classic Book of Zen Koans* (Boston: Wisdom Publications, 2004), 70.

[2] Three I recommend in particular are Kōun, *Gateless Gate*; Shibayama Zenkei, *Gateless Barrier: Zen Comments on the Mumonkan* (**Boston**: Shambhala Publications, 2000); and Robert Aitken, *The Gateless Barrier: Wumenkuan (Mumonkan)* (New York: North Point Press, 1991).

[3] Its longer title is the Heart of the Perfection of Wisdom Sutra (*Prajna-paramita-hrdaya-sutra* in Sanskrit).

[4] I am grateful to John P. Keenan, *The Gospel of Mark: A Mahayana Reading* (Maryknoll, NY: Orbis Books, 1992), for this insight into emptiness as represented by the wilderness in Jesus' experience.

[5] *"Numquam se minus solum quam cum solus esset"* (Cicero, DeOfficiis 3.1).

[6] This notion of the "kindom of God" is based upon a proposal by the late *mujerista* theologian Ada María Isasi-Díaz, and has now come into popular usage in Christian theological circles.

[7] This preferential option for the poor is echoed in the social teaching of the church as articulated and practiced by Christian communities through the ages. See Charles Curran and Richard McCormick, *Official Catholic Social Teaching: Readings in Moral Theology* (Mahwah, NJ: Paulist Press, 1986). Also, for pointed and challenging theological reflections on the issue of Christians and the poor, I recommend Joerg Rieger, *Remember the Poor: Theological Challenge for the Twenty-First Century* (New York: Bloomsbury T&T Clark, 1998), a powerful work that delivers its message described in the subtitle, offering not only a theological challenge but, more important, a challenge for living an authentic human and Christian life as well.

[8] Kōun, *Gateless Gate*, 53.

[9] This appears in Chin-Ning Chu, *The Asian Mind Game: Unlocking the Hidden Agenda of the Asian Business Culture—A Westerner's Survival Manual* (New York: Macmillan, 1991), 182.

# PART FOUR

# UNION

*Although it proclaims "no reliance on words or letters,"*
*thus disclaiming any doctrinal commitment or belief system*
*as a prerequisite for engaging in its practice, Zen tradition*
*nevertheless takes a fundamental principle in Mahayana*
*Buddhism as a presupposition that undergirds the entire path*
*of practice. This principle is the affirmation that "all sentient*
*beings are all originally endowed with Buddha nature." In*
*the words of the Song of Hakuin, a chant that practitioners*
*often recite in community, "All sentient beings are Buddhas*
*right from the start." To accept this statement as one begins*
*practice is to profess Great Trust, or faith, in the Buddhas,*
*in the ancestors, and in the practice itself. In this sense, the*
*stage of Union is not one that begins only after one has at-*
*tained a certain level of realization in one's practice but is*
*the very underlying dimension of the entire path of practice.*
*We are enlightened even before we start. But, we ask, how*
*so? How can this deluded and fallible being who I am be*
*enlightened already?*

*This Great Doubt spurs us on to the Great Resolve to*
*engage in earnest practice. Undergoing the stages of Purifi-*
*cation and Illumination as described earlier, at some point*

*we may eventually come to appreciate this fundamental affirmation. This can be called the "formal" entry into the stage of Union. In Zen terms, Union means embodying the path of awakening in every facet of one's daily life, from waking up in the morning through the entire day and night.*

*In the Ignatian Exercises, the stage of Union is ushered in with the Third Week—as we join Jesus in his suffering and die with him on the cross—and the Fourth Week—where we experience the rising and awakening to the newness of life with the risen One. This stage of Union is capped by the experience of unconditional Love poured to us from a divine source, opening us to a life lived no longer for selfish interests but to one totally dedicated to simply giving back the unconditional Love to all, in a life of selfless service.*

# 10

# Dying, You Destroy Our Death

When you have attained your self-nature,
You can free yourself from the cycle of birth and death.
How would you free yourself from the cycle of birth
   and death
When the light of your eyes is falling to the ground?
(Tosotsu's Three Barriers, no. 2, from the *Miscellaneous
   Koans*)[1]

The point of Zen is to realize our true nature, also called
our self-nature. We have called this the Principle and Foundation of the Zen life: to experience in a most intimate and
direct way the answer to the questions, "Who am I?" and
"Why am I here?" In being graced with such an experience,
Master Tosotsu tells us, "You can free yourself from the cycle
of birth and death." In short, we are able to free ourselves
from the delusive concepts of our conventional thinking
that tells us that birth ends in death, that death is the end of
life, or that life and death are in opposition to one another.

This koan, the second of Tosotsu's "three barriers"—or
better, three gateways to the world of freedom—is presented
to a Zen practitioner who has been confirmed in having had
an initial glimpse of that world, as a way of further deepening the experience of the world of freedom.

The Zen teacher confronts the student: "All right, if you have realized your true nature and have come to know the answer to the question of who you are and why you are here, now present to me how you would free yourself from birth and death, at that point when you are about to die [this is what is meant by the clause 'when the light of your eyes is falling to the ground']?"

One could imagine being on one's deathbed at a ripe old age, surrounded by family and loved ones, saying good-bye to each one of them individually, and then quietly breathing one's last. Or one could imagine dying suddenly in an unexpected event . . . a traffic accident, an airplane crash, a fall from a cliff, or drowning in the sea. One might die violently by gunfire. Master Tosotsu asks us, "At that very moment, how will you free yourself from the shackles of delusion associated with life and death?"

In being confronted with this question by the Zen teacher, if a student stands up, arms outstretched, and shouts, "Ta-da!" or "Look, I'm alive!" or something to that effect, then the student hasn't broken through the barrier. "Go back and sit some more, and taste the true impact of this koan more deeply," the student would be told.

This koan invites the practitioner to a face-to-face confrontation with death itself, to look the reality of death straight in the eye and experience what comes *just as it is*: the loneliness, the terror in realizing one is facing extinction, or the pain and inconsolable grief in the death of a loved one—the gnawing pain that a cherished one will no longer be around.[2]

The Third Week of the Spiritual Exercises is about following Jesus through his suffering at the hands of his captors, to his death on the cross. Our contemplative exercises have brought us to a deeper appreciation of and experiential encounter with Jesus, no longer seen from a distance in time and space as the itinerant son-of-a-Jewish-carpenter-turned-rabbi who roamed around Palestine two thousand years ago, but as the One who most intimately represents our own true self, who shows us the Way of being awakened in the here and now. Sitting in silence and paying attention to the breath, allowing the stillness to pervade, we let our mind rest in the vast expanse of the universe. From a standpoint beyond time and space, in the eternal here and now, we fix our gaze on Jesus and allow the Way to open its vast horizons to us. Now is the time to follow Jesus through a major turning point of the spiritual path.

## The Last Supper

> While they were eating, Jesus took a loaf of bread, and after blessing it he broke it, gave it to the disciples, and said, "Take, eat; this is my body." Then he took a cup, and after giving thanks he gave it to them, saying, "Drink from it, all of you; for this is my blood of the covenant, which is poured out for many for the forgiveness of sins." (Matt. 26:26–28)

Matthew depicts Jesus as fully cognizant of what is about to happen to him from this point on, aware of his impending death. In this state of mind he calls his disciples together for a meal.

"*While they were eating*": A meal with friends and loved ones can be an intimate and sacred experience. Nowadays, with fast foods and cafeteria-style meals where individuals line up to take what they want, take a seat to munch it up, and then leave for the next thing on their schedule, those precious moments of taking a meal in the company of loved ones and friends, regrettably, are largely missed. But every now and then we may still be able to reclaim and relish such occasions of sacredness and intimacy, as we gather with family or friends for a good home-cooked meal. Such occasions are truly a time for celebrating, a time for thanksgiving for the gifts we are to one another.

*"Jesus took bread":* Bread is the staple food in many countries; in others, it may be rice or another grain, potato, or yucca. The bread that we eat every day is the marvelous outcome of many factors:

- The wondrous processes of nature that enable the seed to sprout into seedlings and be nurtured by the sun, the rain, the earth, and all the organisms in the soil to become the wheat stalks that bring forth the sheaves
- The work of human hands that harvested them, threshed them, husked them, and stored them in the warehouse
- The efforts of the truck drivers who transported them across long distances to reach the bakeries where they would be kneaded into dough by the bakers who put them into their large ovens and took them out hot and fresh ready for delivery to the grocery stores
- The loving hands of the mother or father who bought the bread (or baked their own) to be set on the table for the family.

All these interconnected factors make this piece of bread what it is: food for the world.

*"He broke it and gave it to his disciples, saying, 'Take and eat'":* The bread cannot be eaten and become our nourishment unless it is broken into pieces and given to us. Jesus hands it over, piece by piece, to those taking the meal with him, for them to eat, for their nourishment.

*"This is my body":* What is "this" when Jesus says, "This

is my body"? We are invited to look closely at this act that accompanies these words. Jesus is making an offering with this bread in hand, broken, handing it over to his friends to eat. Let us look at this act with the eyes of our heart, and sit with it, breathe with it, and let it sink in. *This* is my body.

Let us look at this bread being handed over. This bread is what it is with the multitude of interconnected factors that have been gathered together from all over the world and handed over for us to eat. Everything in the whole world, in all their wondrous interconnections, comes together in this piece of bread. *This* is my *body*.

My Zen teacher, Yamada Kōun, gives an account of an experience he had while riding on a train from Tokyo to his home in Kamakura, reading a book by thirteenth-century Zen master Dogen. Kōun came upon a passage that read, "The Mind is no other than mountains and rivers, the great wide earth, the sun, the moon, the stars." At that moment, all of a sudden, something hit him like lightning, and he burst out laughing. But since he was in a public place, he tried to muffle it and restrain himself. His wife, who was sitting beside him, and who did not know what was going on, also urged him to quiet down and not make a scene. He comported himself soberly for the time being, stepped off the train at their station, took a taxi home with his wife, and went ahead with dinner and then rest for the evening. Then, he writes,

At midnight, I abruptly awakened. At first my mind was foggy, then suddenly that quotation flashed into my consciousness. "I came to realize clearly that Mind is no other than mountains, rivers, and the great wide earth, the sun and the moon and the stars." And I repeated it. Then all at once I was struck as though by lightning, and the next instant heaven and earth crumbled and disappeared. Instantaneously, like surging waves, a tremendous delight welled up in me, a veritable hurricane of delight, as I laughed loudly and wildly: "Ha ha ha ha ha ha ha! There's no reasoning here, no reasoning at all! Ha ha ha!" The empty sky split in two, then opened its enormous mouth and began to laugh uproariously, Ha ha ha! Later, one of the members of my family told me that my laughter had sounded inhuman.[3]

This well-cited enlightenment experience changed the life of one Japanese business executive and opened up his life to make him one of the great Zen masters of the twentieth century.[4] What is referred to as "mind" in the English translation here is the character pronounced as "*hsin*" in Chinese, or "*kokoro*" in Japanese, referring not just to the intellectual faculty but to the very core of our being, the "heart of the matter." The term refers to the most intimate place within myself whereby I am most truly who I am. Zen Master Dogen writes that the most intimate place within myself is "no other than mountains, rivers, and the great wide earth, the sun and the moon and the stars." I am that. *This is my body.*

Who is saying, "This is my body"? Here, the lines that separate me and you and Jesus have disappeared. There is no specific entity that could claim that this is "my" body, mine and mine alone. In Buddhist terms, this word has now become an empty "my," and is simply that, in all clarity and glory and splendor: *This is my body*—all glory and splendor, yes, but broken, nevertheless, with the shadow of the cross looming over it.

This scene of the Last Supper is reenacted by Christians when they get together for worship in a ceremony, commemoration, and celebration known as the Eucharist. This term is from the Greek, meaning "to give thanks." Followers of Jesus throughout the world gather together to give thanks, offer prayers, and share a ceremonial meal. The high point of the gathering is when the priest, as the representative of Jesus, takes the bread, lifts it up before everyone, and proclaims, "This is my body."

Soon after, everyone is invited to come up to the altar and receive the bread, in the same way that was done at the Last Supper. The bread has just been received, tasted, chewed (unless it is a wafer that melts in the mouth), and swallowed, absorbed into one's own body. *This is my body.* Let this be heard in the stillness, and let it permeate throughout the entire body of those gathered together in that celebration—and wider, throughout the entire world and all the living beings therein—and wider still, through the mountains, rivers, the sun, the moon, and stars.

*"After giving thanks"*: Recognizing all these interconnected factors that make this bread what it is, the most natural sentiment that comes forth is to give thanks. And as we look around us, at each and every thing that we take as food, use as implements, or wear as clothing, the same sentiment wells up. We are indebted to all the elements of the universe, and all the living beings, human and nonhuman, that, by being what they are and doing what they do, give us these things we eat, use, and wear, and thus allow us to be who we are. As we open our eyes to all these levels of interconnectedness, we realize how we are immersed in a wondrous communion with all, in simply being who we are, as we are.

This deep sense of gratitude (*eucharist*, from the Greek, as noted above), based on a palpable experience of interconnectedness with all, becomes a constant in our day-to-day lives. We are able to meet any situation with a heart of generosity and equanimity.

### In the Garden of Gethsemane

> Then Jesus went with them to a place called Gethsemane, and he said to his disciples, "Sit here while I go over there and pray." (Matt. 26:36)

*Sit here.* This is all we are asked to do. Let us pay attention here and put our entire lives at stake in this. *Just this, this very moment.* Breath by breath, we are invited to take in the momentous impact of all that this entails. Time stops, the world stops turning. Just this, here, now. Then Jesus says, "I am deeply grieved, even to death." Jesus is with his friends, but they are oblivious to what is going on with him. He feels all the more alone, confronted and struggling in agony with the thought of his own impending death.

In the rock opera *Jesus Christ Superstar*, the scene in the garden of Gethsemane is presented dramatically, with the Jesus character crying out at the top of his voice, "Why must I die?" His inner struggle and agony reverberate throughout the audience, as this pointed question is raised emphatically, as if to invite all of us listeners to join in: "Why must I die?"

Coming face to face with the fact of our own mortality is a crucial point in our journey through this earthly life. This contemplation of Jesus' agony in the garden is a precious occasion for a face-to-face confrontation with our own death. Master Tosotsu's glaring eyes loom large in front of us, with his question lunging at our hearts: "How would you free yourself from the cycle of birth and death," when you are about to die? Behold how Jesus struggles with this moment, to the point of his sweat becoming "like great drops of blood falling down on the ground" (Luke 22:44). He experiences fear, in utter loneliness and powerlessness, near desperation, crying out from the depths. Take the invitation:

sit with Jesus right there in the middle of all this. Be with Jesus now, through his agony in the garden, about to face certain death. Put yourself in his place. It is also your own death that this contemplative exercise is about. Continue breathing with this thought in the stillness.

Ramana Maharsi, known in his youth by the name Venkataramanan, who lost his father in his early teens, recounts an experience wherein he is suddenly overcome by the fear of death.

I was sitting alone in a room on the first floor of my uncle's house. I seldom had any sickness and on that day there was nothing wrong with my health, but a sudden violent fear of death overtook me. There was nothing in my state of health to account for it nor was there any urge in me to find out whether there was any account for the fear. I just felt I was going to die and began thinking what to do about it. It did not occur to me to consult a doctor or any elders or friends. I felt I had to solve the problem myself then and there. The shock of the fear of death drove my mind inwards and I said to myself mentally, without actually framing the words: "Now death has come; what does it mean? What is it that is dying? This body dies." And at once I dramatized the occurrence of death. I lay with my limbs stretched out still as though rigor mortis had set in, and imitated a corpse so as to give greater reality to the enquiry. I held my breath and kept my lips tightly closed so that no sound could escape, and that neither the word "I" nor any word could be uttered. "Well, then," I said to myself, "this body is dead. It will be carried stiff to the burning ground and there burn and be reduced to ashes. But with the death of the body, am I dead? Is the body I? It is silent and inert, but I feel the full force of my personality and even the voice of I within me, apart from it. So I am the Spirit transcending the body. The body dies but the spirit transcending it cannot be touched by death. That means I am the deathless Spirit." All this was not dull thought; it flashed through me vividly as living truths which I perceived directly almost without thought process. I was something real, the only real thing about my present state, and all the conscious activity connected with the body was centered on that I. From that moment onwards, the "I" or Self focused attention on itself by a powerful fascination. Fear of death vanished once and for all. The ego was lost in the flood of Self-awareness. Absorption in the Self continued unbroken from that time.[5]

What the young Venkataramanan does is to brace himself and take a straight look at this death in the face, opening his heart and surrendering to it. What ensues is the momentous turning point of his life. "Fear of death vanished once and for all. The ego was lost in the flood of Self-Awareness . . . and continued unbroken from that time."

*"Father, if you are willing, remove this cup from me; not my will, but yours be done"*: Jesus, confronting his impending death and having struggled with this from the very depths of his being, surrenders his own will to the Father's. In this act of total surrender he finds liberation. He is now filled with deep peace and equanimity.

Again in the rock opera *Jesus Christ Superstar*, after his struggles, Jesus comes to a standstill and pauses in a moment of silence. He stands up, serenely, and utters, "To conquer death, you only have to die. You only have to die." He has now come to terms with the fact of his impending death, and he is free. Though still in the midst of uncertainty, knowing he will still have to undergo severe pain and torture as they nail him on the cross, he is in deep peace. Here is the hint for seeing through the koan in Tosotsu's *Three Barriers*, which asks (paraphrased): "How would you free yourself from the cycle of birth and death, at that point when you are about to die?"

In surrendering his little self, or "my will," to the Father and accepting his own death, Jesus is at one with his True Self and is free. From here all the rest is just letting things follow their course in total freedom. The events that follow eventually lead to Jesus being sentenced to death, being falsely accused before the religious authorities and the political rulers, exposed as a criminal before the populace, sentenced to death, and subjected to abject humiliation and physical torture. He is executed in the mode that was customary at the time, being hung on a wooden cross, and left to suffocate in excruciating pain. We are invited to behold the Man on the cross, at the point of death. Sit with this in stillness, and let it sink in.

*"My God, My God, why have you forsaken me?" (Matt. 27:46):* This is a cry from the depths of our being as we find ourselves placed in situations of unbearable pain and suffering. As we gaze at our own human condition, our eyes are opened to the fact that so many of our fellow human beings utter this cry from the depths, in the various situations to which they are consigned.

Countless people die of plague, famine, fire, earthquake, tsunami, and natural or human-made disasters. So much violence has been perpetrated by human beings against one another in so many different forms, throughout history and continuing in our twenty-first-century world. So many instances of intentional and organized human violence that we hear in the news or read about in the papers make us shudder to the core of our being. Put yourself in the place of one of the victims of these unspeakable atrocities. *My God, my God, why have you forsaken me?*

In our own individual journeys, we are also placed in situations where this cry wells up from the core of our being. A mother loses her two-year-old son by accidental drowning in a family pool. A father is in deep grief for his twelve-year-old son, his only child, who commits suicide in desperation after persistent bullying at school. A working single mother with two young children is fired from her job, and she also finds out that she has advanced ovarian cancer. A thirty-year-old man is accused and convicted of a rape he did not commit, and through a flawed investigation and a faulty justice system he is sentenced to life in prison. These and innumerable other kinds of human situations bring us to our wit's end and can happen to any of us, bringing forth the cry, *My God, my God, why have you forsaken me!*

I was visiting my home country, the Philippines, from Japan, where I had been assigned to work as a Jesuit priest, and a Catholic nun I met at a Zen retreat had offered to take me to Tondo, a poor urban district in Manila where she served in various capacities: social worker, community organizer, animator, Bible study leader, and go-between of sorts. We entered a shack among the many made with plywood and makeshift material in which most of the people in this area lived. In the middle of the crowded room with bright lights all over was a small coffin, and therein lay the dead body of a two-year-old girl, surrounded by her grieving family and visiting neighbors. I learned from the conversations there that the little girl had already been in a malnourished state, compounded by some form of skin disease that had made her itch all over, when she caught a cold that turned into pneumonia. She died as a result of it. *My God, why have you forsaken me!*

As we behold the figure of Jesus on the cross, we breathe deeply, in and out, descend into the silence, and allow the stillness to reign. As we lose ourselves in the stillness, we hear the cry that emerges from the depths, in unison with all those who were there at Auschwitz; in Nanjing, Hiroshima, and Nagasaki; all the victims of Stalin, Mao, Pol Pot, and all the despots in history; in solidarity with all those who, in the depths of their own suffering and desperation, uttered the cry, *My God, my God, why have you forsaken me?* As we open our heart and absorb this condition in our own being in the depths of the silence, we see that the cry of every man, woman, and child who ever lived and experienced their own suffering is the cry of Jesus on the cross.

Some years ago, during a car ride at one of our annual meetings of the American Zen Teachers' Association, I was in a spirited conversation about religion, spirituality, and related matters with a Zen teacher from another lineage, who came to Zen practice from a Jewish background but who no longer identified with that tradition. Knowing of my Christian background and practice, she asked me in a pointed yet friendly sort of way, "So why did Jesus have to die on the cross?" In the context of our conversation I understood that she had in mind the received Christian idea of Jesus' death on the cross in order to atone for the sins of humankind, but she could not quite figure out how Christians could believe in a God who would let his own Son die in that cruel way to pay off the sins of everyone else. She just could not buy into that idea of such a God in the first place, nor of Jesus as the Son of God who died in a supreme sacrifice of his life to atone for the sins of all of humankind.

As I was about to begin a long-winded, theologically based response, we were told we had just arrived at our destination, so I was not able to continue. I never had the chance to follow up on that conversation.

What I was attempting to do at the time, taking a Christian theological standpoint, was to suggest in my fumbling words that perhaps, just perhaps, it might make more sense to say not that Jesus the Son of God died on the cross *for* all of humankind but that he died *with* all of humankind. In short, in the figure of the Beloved One, dying on the cross and maligned by the people around as a common criminal, the cry of "My God, my God, why have you forsaken me?" can convey an entirely different message about God's place in all this.

Indeed, why did Jesus have to die on the cross? This question resonates in the same way as, Why did more than 6 million Jews have to die at the hands of the Nazis during World War II? Why do twenty-one thousand children under the age of five, on all continents, have to die of hunger and malnutrition each day in today's world? Why do tens of thousands of people, many of them vacationers spending time at a beach, many of them residents living close to the ocean going about their normal business, die as they are swept away by the waters of a massive tsunami? Why do more than three thousand people who are in their offices for a regular day of work in two tall buildings in New York City have to die, as planes hijacked by a group of men with a murderous intent carry out their plot? Why does a young mother of thirty-one die of cancer, leaving her loving husband and one-year-old son? Why does a youth of eighteen on a study tour in Europe have to die accidentally, electrocuted by a live wire on a train car stopped on the railroad tracks in the middle of the night while frolicking with friends? Why do twenty-seven innocent people, most of them young children under the age of seven or eight, have to die of gunshot wounds from a weapon wielded by a young man who goes on a violent rampage? Why does a young woman have to die after being raped by a band of men who were in a night bus she happened to take with her boyfriend in a city in India? The list is endless, as long as the list of the names of humanity itself. Why? Why? Why? *My God, my God, why have you forsaken me?* The cry is heard from the depths as we sit there in stillness.

We become one in this cry, from the depths of our broken hearts, in unison with all our fellow human beings who have ever lived, suffered, and died. But dwelling in the stillness, with broken hearts grieving with all our fellow human beings at the point of their death, the cry, "My God, my God, why have you forsaken me?" remains in the background, as another one wells out of that same place of stillness with a gentle whisper in our hearts: *You are not alone. Behold, I am with you. You are my beloved, with whom I am well pleased.*

We are invited to remain immersed in the depths of stillness through all this. As we do, Master Tosotsu's eyes glare at us, and his voice from the koan nudges at us: "How will you free yourself from the cycle of birth and death when the light of your eyes is falling to the ground?"

*"Father, forgive them; for they do not know what they are doing" (Luke 23:34):* Though he is innocent Jesus has been falsely accused, arrested and tortured, and condemned to death. How many times have we felt that we have been misunderstood, maligned, treated unfairly, or deprived of what we feel is our due? Jesus' words invite us to look at our accusers or tormentors, those who have misunderstood or maligned us or treated us unfairly; breathe with them; and put ourselves in their place.

In Tibetan Buddhist practice, a particular form of meditative exercise is called "exchange of self and other."[6] This exercise has several levels, involving visualization and imagination—putting oneself in the place of other persons, including loved ones, deemed "inferior" and "superior" to oneself (in terms of age, social or economic standing, or other external criteria). This meditation can also be employed when we find ourselves in situations of being wronged or unjustly treated. We place ourselves in the shoes of the person or persons who have caused us harm or suffering and see things from that perspective. In this way, we are able to expand our horizon and welcome into our hearts with compassion those persons we would otherwise resent or hate, or upon whom we would seek revenge.

Jesus' prayer, "Father, forgive them; for they don't know what they are doing," is an actualization of this exchange of self and other, and thereby breaks through the separation that divides perpetrator and victim, washing both in the cleansing waters of compassion and forgiveness.

*"Father, into your hands I commend my spirit" (Luke 23:46):* At this moment, Jesus sums up his entire life and completes it just as it began. That Spirit has drawn him forth and led him throughout his earthly life, empowering him to do everything that he ever did. And now it is time to conclude his life on earth, with this one great act of entrustment, giving the Breath back to its Source.

This act is simply the culmination of all the acts of entrustment, with every breath, given throughout his life, through every moment of it. This entrustment upon the Breath sums up Jesus' entire life, making Jesus all that he was, all that he is, all that he will be for all of us.

The Great Trust that we began with in launching into the Zen path is also what leads us and guides us every step along the way. In entrusting ourselves to the same Breath, we become the true self that each of us really is. In giving ourselves entirely in trust to the Breath, we die to self and open ourselves to live in the newness of life empowered by that same Breath.

### Notes

[1]This collection of koans is given to Zen practitioners in the Sanbo Kyodan lineage, as a way of polishing an initial glimpse of the Way—"the world of our true nature" with which a seeker may be graced in the course of Zen practice.

[2]I thank dharma brother Greg Mayers, who has gone through the throes of what was diagnosed as terminal cancer and lived through it, for his precious comments related to this point.

[3]Philip Kapleau, ed., *The Three Pillars of Zen*, exp. ed. (New York: Anchor Books, 1980), 216.

[4]See Yamada Kōun, *The Gateless Gate* (Boston: Wisdom Publications, 2004).

[5]Arthur Osborne, *The Mind of Ramana Maharshi* (Mumbai: Jaico Publishing House, 1959), 7-8.

[6]From chapter 8 of Shantideva's *Guide to the Bodhisattva Path*. A recommended edition, with commentary, is Pema Chodron, *No Time to Lose: A Timely Guide to the Way of the Bodhisattva* (Boston: Shambhala Publications, 2007).

# 11

# Arise, Be Awake!

## *Back to Galilee*

Once you have freed yourself from the cycle of birth and death, you know where to go. After you have died, and are buried, where are you going? (Tosotsu's Three Barriers, no. 3)

The third of Master Tosotsu's Three Barriers probes further into our inner being, checking our degree of freedom. If indeed you have been freed from the delusions of life and death, you know where you are going from here. You are now dead and buried (or cremated, as you may have stipulated in your will), and some time has elapsed. So now, where are you going? This is a momentous question for each of us as we grapple with the mystery of life itself. Where do we go after we die?

The religions of the world have their own particular answers to this big question of our human existence. Greek mythology has its images of the Elysian fields on the one hand, and Hades on the other, as destinations for those who have departed from this world. The notion of *sheol* appears in Hebrew Scriptures as a dark place where the dead go.

And of course, we have the Christian concepts of heaven and hell, and purgatory in between.

The traditional Hindu view posits six realms of existence within this world of *samsara*, or the cycle of birth and death, and one's karmic residue determines to which realm one will go in the next life. The Buddhist view adapted the basic Hindu framework and added four more levels, the tenth and highest realm being that of the Buddhas, or those who have reached nirvana and who will never again be reborn into this cycle of birth and death.

Other religious traditions have other views of the afterlife, which can serve as a backdrop for presenting a response to Master Tosotsu's penetrating question: "After you have died, and are buried, where are you going?"

The Zen practitioner is enjoined to go deep into that place of stillness and let an authentic response come out in all clarity from that place. When it does, it is like a lightning bolt that brightens the heavens.

Let me offer some scenarios based on this koan for the seeker grappling with this question, "Where will I go after I die?"

Yasutani Hakuun Rōshi, the teacher of Yamada Kōun—who was my teacher—is said to have given this response to the third item of Master Tosotsu: "I will go where my karma takes me." In giving this response, he was presupposing the Buddhist framework of ten realms of beings and is saying something like, "If I have done such evil things in this life that will need to be punished and atoned for in hell, then I will go there. If I die with some unfulfilled longing or craving, then I will go to the realm of the hungry ghosts. If I die with resentment or ill will toward other beings, I will go to the realm of the malignant spirits. If I have done meritorious acts that merit birth in the heavenly realm, there I will go."

The underlying point is: wherever I am destined to go, I am at peace with it and will accept my destiny.

This answer comes from a heart that has found true inner peace and equanimity, indicating that one is now fully at home in the universe, wherever one may be. This total peace of mind can be said to be one of the vital fruits of Zen practice sustained through the years.

Yasutani Rōshi's answer is suitable for offering in a public forum, like a dharma talk for practitioners or seekers in general. In a one-to-one encounter between practitioner and teacher, one is invited to plumb a deeper level and offer another kind of response. This response comes from the very depths, so intimate to oneself that one cannot share it openly with others. This is a response coming out of that place of deep inner peace and equanimity, with the power of wiping away all one's delusions and anxieties about one's ultimate destiny. Contemplative exercises on the scenes of the risen One may also offer us some guidance in this direction.

## Back to Galilee

Jesus is dead; long live Jesus! Where has Jesus gone? The death of Jesus is precisely the passageway that ushers in the risen One in our midst. This message—he is risen!—is at the heart of Christian faith itself, without which, as Paul says, everything else we believe and all the things we do as Christians will be in vain. The Fourth and concluding Week of the Spiritual Exercises invites us to contemplate this point in order to shed light on our entire lives going forward.

The Gospel of Mark records the scenario after the death of Jesus:

When the sabbath was over, Mary Magdalene, and Mary the mother of James, and Salome bought spices, so that they might go and anoint him. And very early on the first day of the week, when the sun had risen, they went to the tomb. They had been saying to one another, "Who will roll away the stone for us from the entrance to the tomb?" When they looked up, they saw that the stone, which was very large, had already been rolled back. As they entered the tomb, they saw a young man, dressed in a white robe, sitting on the right side; and they were alarmed. But he said to them, "Do not be alarmed; you are looking for Jesus of Nazareth, who was crucified. He has been raised; he is not here. Look, there is the place they laid him. But go, tell his disciples and Peter that he is going ahead of you to Galilee; there you will see him, just as he told you." So they went out and fled from the tomb, for terror and amazement had seized them; and they said nothing to anyone, for they were afraid. (Mark 16:1–8)

The key point for our focus here is the injunction, "He is going ahead of you to Galilee. There you will see him, just as he told you." What is the significance of this?

A first question is, why Galilee? Galilee represents the everyday life with which the followers of Jesus are familiar. It is where they were born, grew up, found their work, nurtured their families, and lived the ups and downs of human life. It is where they get up in the morning, wash their face, take their breakfast, go to work, return home, take a rest, and so on. On the one hand, Galilee represents the humdrum of day to day, but on the other, it is precisely the place in which the risen One, the Holy One, comes to be manifest in us.

Feminist and mujerista theologians in the United States refer to *lo cotidiano*, a Spanish word for "the everyday," which Maria Pilar Aquino describes as the "whole of doing and thinking of our people in their daily lives and recurring routine."[1] In the midst of the everyday, the Divine enters our lives and liberates us from the oppressive conditions of our humdrum existence, if we but open our eyes to see. This is the Galilee that Jesus invites us to return to—our everyday lives—and thereby be in the presence of the risen One.

Luke offers a similar message in his first chapter of the Acts of the Apostles.

> While he was going and they were gazing up toward heaven, suddenly two men in white robes stood by them. They said, "Men of Galilee, why do you stand looking up toward heaven? This Jesus, who has been taken up from you into heaven, will come in the same way as you saw him go into heaven." (Acts 1:11)

Here the scene is about the ascension of the risen One into heaven, and the followers of Jesus have a tendency to turn their gaze upward, looking at the beyond, or the afterlife in heaven. But the messenger tells them, the people of Galilee, to turn their gaze back earthward and return to their human tasks in Galilee, as it is there that Jesus will come back.

### Breaking Bread Together

Luke has another account of the risen One that can also be eye-opening for us, as it was for the interlocutors in the narrative. Luke tells the famous story of the two travelers going to Emmaus:

> Now on that same day two of them were going to a village called Emmaus, about seven miles from Jerusalem, and talking with each other about all these things that had happened. While they were talking and discussing, Jesus himself came near and went with them,

but their eyes were kept from recognizing him. And he said to them, "What are you discussing with each other while you walk along?" They stood still, looking sad. Then one of them, whose name was Cleopas, answered him, "Are you the only stranger in Jerusalem who does not know the things that have taken place there in these days?" He asked them, "What things?" They replied, "The things about Jesus of Nazareth, who was a prophet mighty in deed and word before God and all the people, and how our chief priests and leaders handed him over to be condemned to death and crucified him. But we had hoped that he was the one to redeem Israel. Yes, and besides all this, it is now the third day since these things took place. Moreover, some women of our group astounded us. They were at the tomb early this morning, and when they did not find his body there, they came back and told us that they had indeed seen a vision of angels who said that he was alive. Some of those who were with us went to the tomb and found it just as the women had said; but they did not see him." Then he said to them, "Oh, how foolish you are, and how slow of heart to believe all that the prophets have declared! Was it not necessary that the Messiah should suffer these things and then enter into his glory?" Then beginning with Moses and all the prophets, he interpreted to them the things about himself in all the scriptures. As they came near the village to which they were going, he walked ahead as if he were going on. But they urged him strongly, saying, "Stay with us, because it is almost evening and the day is now nearly over." So he went in to stay with them. When he was at the table with them, he took bread, blessed and broke it, and gave it to them. Then their eyes were opened, and they recognized him; and he vanished from their sight. They said to each other, "Were not our hearts burning within us while he was talking to us on the road, while he was opening the scriptures to us?" That same hour they got up and returned to Jerusalem; and they found the eleven and their companions gathered together. They were saying, "The Lord has risen indeed, and he has appeared to Simon!" Then they told what had happened on the road, and how he had been made known to them in the breaking of the bread. (Luke 24:13–35)

We are the travelers in this journey of our earthly life, and open our hearts to one another and to those we encounter along the road. We share our desires and longings, our joys and hopes, and find solace in one another's company. But if we are focused only on our own narrow little worlds, our eyes are blocked from seeing, and we fail to recognize the One who walks with us every step along the way. We are thus enjoined to sit down and relax, cherish one another's company, be grateful for the gift that we are to one another, and share a meal.

The "breaking of the bread" refers on one level to the Eucharistic meal that Jesus instituted, when his followers gather together regularly in worship and thanksgiving. The Eucharist becomes an occasion to recognize that the risen One is in our midst, and that we are in the midst of the risen One, as the Gospel of Matthew says, "Where two or three are gathered in my name, I am there among them" (Matt. 18:20). But on another level, the level of *lo cotidiano*, breaking bread may also be in the simple, everyday event of sharing a meal together with friends and family, during which we are invited to open the eyes of our hearts and recognize that, as we do, we are on sacred ground, in the presence of the Holy One.

## The Least of These

Where else may we be able to recognize the risen One? Another passage from Matthew offers a hint.

"When the Son of Man comes in his glory, and all the angels with him, then he will sit on the throne of his glory. All the nations will be gathered before him, and he will separate people one from another as a shepherd separates the sheep from the goats, and he will put the sheep at his right hand and the goats at the left. Then the king will say to those at his right hand, 'Come, you that are blessed by my Father, inherit the kingdom prepared for you from the foundation of the world; for I was hungry and you gave me food, I was thirsty and you gave me something to drink, I was a stranger and you welcomed me, I was naked and you gave me clothing, I was sick and you took care of me, I was in prison and you visited me.' Then the righteous will answer him, 'Lord, when was it that we saw you hungry and gave you food, or thirsty and gave you something to drink? And when was it that we saw you a stranger and welcomed you, or naked and gave you clothing? And when was it that we saw you sick or in prison and visited you?' And the king will answer them, 'Truly I tell you, just as you did it to one of the least of these who are members of my family, you did it to me.'" (Matt. 25:31–40)

This passage is often (mis)read as a moral injunction and a promise of reward, that is, "to feed the hungry, give drink to the thirsty, be kind to the stranger," so that "you may be worthy of inheriting the kingdom." The text is also often cited as a motivation for much that Christians have done in history: precisely to help the poor, feed the hungry, and welcome the stranger. In doing so, they would thus merit their heavenly reward.

Such a reading may be an incentive for Christians to do good things on behalf of others but would seem to miss an important point. Note that those welcomed into the kingdom were not seeking any reward, heavenly or otherwise, when they offered food to the hungry and drink to the thirsty. To do such charitable acts with a view to being rewarded demeans the act itself, as well as the person or persons on behalf of whom one is doing the good deed. By that very fact, such an action would thereby not be deemed worthy of the reward but can even be seen as an act of selfishness on a higher level, using the other as a ploy or instrument for one's desire to gain merit in heaven.

How can we get to the deeper message of the passage? "The least of these who are members of my family" is our key here.[2] As we open our hearts to the least of these, we will find the risen One present and alive in our midst. The reward is in the very act itself, in opening our hearts to the least of these no less to one another—to each person whom we meet in this journey of life, and continuing to walk together every step along the way.

Living in such a way, open-hearted in welcoming our neighbor into our hearts, and being transformed accordingly, we may be surprised by joy.[3] Behold, the risen One is among us!

### Notes

[1] Maria Pilar Aquino, "Theological Method in U.S. Latino/a Theology," in *From the Heart of Our People: Latino/a Explorations in Catholic Systematic Theology*, ed. Orlando Espin and Miguel Diaz (Maryknoll, NY: Orbis Books, 1999), 38.

[2]I recommend a book by Elaine Heath, *We Were the Least of These: Reading the Bible with Survivors of Sexual Abuse* (Ada, MI: Brazos Press, 2011), for further light on this theme of resurrection, in opening horizons for healing and liberation in the midst of unspeakably painful human situations.

[3]With grateful acknowledgment to C. S. Lewis, *Surprised by Joy: The Shape of My Early Life*, rev. ed. (Boston: Houghton Mifflin Roughcourt, 1995).

## 12

# Basking in Divine Love

## *The Eyes and Hands of Kuan-yin*

Ungan asked Dôgo, "What does the Bodhisattva of the Great Compassion use so many hands and eyes for?" (*Blue Cliff Records*, no. 89)[1]

In the practice of Zen, as we sit still, we are enjoined to take each breath as if it were our first, at the same time breathing as if the breath were our last. With this attitude we welcome each new breath with gratitude and freshness, and each new moment as a new gift of the universe to us, allowing us to throb with life with everything else around. In that stillness I open my eyes and see everything around me—the sun, the moon, the stars, the mountains, the great wide earth—and in it, every pebble, every blade of grass, every sentient being. I behold the wonder and beauty of each and every one, just as it is. Everything is seen in its particularity as a manifestation of that same Love that makes me who I am, and that makes everything what it is.

Sitting still, we are able to behold all that this life entails as intimately interconnected with each and everything else, seeing everything with a sense of awe, wonder, and gratitude. I am able to see everything that has happened in my life, from my infancy through childhood, and on up to this point. I see every encounter therein as a precious gift that has been given, and continues to be poured out, in infinite measure, in unconditional Love.

The figure of Kuan-yin with a thousand eyes and hands embodies this way of beholding the universe with eyes filled with Love, and responding in ways moved by that Love.[2] Kuan-yin is the Bodhisattva of Great Compassion, who sees everything with eyes of wisdom that reveals the interconnectedness of all beings, and who, filled with a heart of compassion, responds by taking skillful means appropriate to each situation.

A message repeated by the ancestors and sages of the Zen tradition is this: Kuan-yin is you! Kuan-yin is none other than each and every one of us. Yet the concerns of the little egoistic self, centered on the I-me-mine, cloud our mind and prevent it from seeing its true self as Kuan-yin. Sitting still and letting the mind rest in that stillness allows the clouds of my mind to be gradually blown away by a gentle wind, and opened up to the clear blue sky enlightened by the noonday sun. In the transparent light of that noonday sun, we are able to see everything just as it is. Each and every thing shines out in its true brilliance.

Case 89 of the *Blue Cliff Records*, whose first line opens our chapter above, refers to Kuan-yin with the thousand hands.

Ungan asked Dôgo, "What does the Bodhisattva of the Great Compassion use so many hands and eyes for?" Dôgo answered, "It is like a person in the middle of the night reaching with his hand behind his head groping for his pillow." Ungan said, "I understood." Dôgo said, "How did you understand it?" Ungan said, "The whole

body is hands and eyes." Dôgo said, "You said it very
well. But you expressed only eight-tenths of it." Ungan
said, "How would you say it, Elder Brother?" Dôgo
said, "The entire body is hands and eyes."[3]

The eyes of Kuan-yin are the eyes of wisdom that see
each and every thing in this universe just as it is, without
distortion or obstruction, precisely as interconnected with
each and everything else. The hands of Kuan-yin are the
hands that respond out of a heart of compassion to the different situations of sentient beings needing assistance and
liberation from various forms of suffering. "Groping for
a pillow in the middle of the night" indicates that there is
no self-consciousness in the actions of Kuan-yin: it offers a
hand in response out of compassion in the most natural and
spontaneous way, having overcome the separation of self
and other. The hands of Kuan-yin offer food to the hungry,
drink to the thirsty, companionship to the lonely, a word of
advice to the confused, a wagging finger or scolding hand
to those who misbehave, and a consoling hand to those
who are forlorn.

"The whole body" is this very body, which thus becomes
the hands and eyes of compassion in its very being. This
body is not just my individual body but the entire universe,
mountains and rivers, the great wide earth, the sun, the
moon, the stars, and all beings who have ever been born or
will be born in this vast universe.

"The eyes and hands of Kuan-yin" is another way of
conveying the unconditional and infinite Love that permeates the entire universe. The path of stillness in Zen and
the path laid out by Ignatius in the Spiritual Exercises are
parallel and intertwining ways of experiencing this infinite
Love in a most intimate way that transforms our entire life.

## A View from the Summit

The inward journey that we take in following the Spiritual Exercises is meant to lead us eventually to the place where the fountains of unconditional Love may gush forth and saturate us in infinite measure. The culminating point of the Exercises is the aptly called "Contemplation on Divine Love." It is the summit from which the entire path laid out by Ignatius in these Spiritual Exercises can be seen in full light—the vantage point from which we are able to behold our entire life in fresh light, seeing it in all its ups and downs, twists and turns, as suffused with unconditional Love right from the very start.

Having undergone the Great Death with Jesus on the cross in the Third Week, Ignatius offers us this contemplative practice in the Fourth Week as a way to arise and awaken to the infinite Life that flows right in the midst of our daily life. In a palpable and irreversible way we come to the realization that we are here on earth because we are loved, and unconditionally so, and that our true joy and purpose in life are to give back the love so abundantly received.

## Life in Communion

Engaging in this contemplative exercise we seek "an interior knowledge" of this unconditional Love that would thereby move us to live our lives as a way of loving back, out of deep gratitude. Ignatius offers two considerations: first, that love is truly manifested in actions rather than in words; second, that love consists in a total sharing of all that we have and all that we are—our "having" as well as our "being." In short, we are not dealing here with a fuzzy sentiment nor a fleeting emotion, but a way of be-ing that naturally flows into all our do-ing. We are invited to enter a way of be-ing that is characterized by an intimate life in communion.

The love we are invited to experience and realize at the depths of our being in this contemplative exercise is not just something that we may be able to feel in certain moments. There may be such precious moments during the contemplation or even in spontaneous and unguarded occasions in daily life when we are precisely inundated with such a feeling of being at the top of the world as we realize ourselves suffused in unconditional Love. The feeling is perhaps better described as a down-to-earth frame of mind, a constant attitude of gazing at everything and everyone with the eyes of love that permeates through and through—being able to live in a way whereby every thought, word, and action is a way of allowing that love to flow out from me toward everyone and everything around me.

### Four Points for Contemplating Divine Love

Ignatius recommends four intertwining points to serve as the focus of this contemplative exercise. These four points are as follows:

1.  The divine gift of the benefits I have received in creation and redemption and in the particular blessings received throughout my own individual life
2.  The divine indwelling in all of creation
3.  Divine action manifested in the works of nature, including the movements of the sun, moon, and stars in the heavens, the grand scenario of all things in the universe and on this earth, where everything follows its natural course

4. The divine source of all good and honorable things we encounter in our course of life, such as justice, truth, and beauty.

The first point, considering divine Love in the blessings of Creation, is an invitation to contemplate the fact of being alive at this moment. I look around and see the things around me—the tree outside my window, the grass growing on the lawn needing to be mowed, the blue sky. I can hear the chirping of the birds and the voices of people from afar. I sip my coffee and smell the aroma, and I taste the toasted bread with butter thinly spread on it. I feel the cool breeze from the open window caressing my skin.

We are invited to take a fresh look at these ordinary things we normally take for granted and see them with new eyes of wonder, awe, and gratitude.

Thornton Wilder's play *Our Town* offers us a moving example of beholding and appreciating the ordinary things of our life with new eyes of wonder, awe, and gratitude. The main character, Emily, is a young woman who dies in childbirth during the course of the play. Before finally entering the realm inhabited by those who have gone before her, she is given an opportunity to come back and relive any given day of her earthly life. She chooses the day of her twelfth birthday, and viewers of the play are thus vicariously led through the events of that day from Emily's enlightened eyes—the perspective of the realm of the dead. Emily laments how we miss the precious gems of each present moment, taking things for granted and not able to taste the eternal significance of each earthly moment. Hers is a powerful message to all of us living day to day in an unawakened way.

Another layer of this contemplative exercise on the first point considers the particular gifts received in my own individual life. I call to mind the particular family I was born to;

those who nurtured me from my childhood; the people and events in my early upbringing, youth, early adulthood, and so on. I consider the persons in my life who have cared for me and loved me in their own particular ways and who have been instrumental in making me who I am today. I humbly receive the love they gave and continue to give, and I behold each and every one of them also with love and gratitude, wishing and praying for their well-being, whether they are still alive or gone from this world.

The second point is to behold things and consider each of them in particular as a manifestation of divine indwelling. As we look at each and every thing around us with the realization that they do not have to be there at all, and that there could have been nothing at all, new light is shed on the fact that they are existing there before me.

"Why are there existing things, rather than nothing?" Twentieth-century philosopher Martin Heidegger's entire work revolved around this question. Asking the question itself evokes the sense of awe and wonder that we can experience in beholding anything that exists, whether a pebble, a shrub, a caterpillar, or a human being. The task of philosophers is to think about the central questions of our human existence and figure out possible answers using conceptual language to the best of their ability.

Reading philosophical works can be thought provoking if we are looking for answers to the question of why there are existing things rather than nothing. But as we read, in the process of forming conceptual structures that seek to explain our mode of being as humans, we tend to diminish and eventually obliterate the sense of awe and wonder that begins with such great promise in asking the question itself. Heidegger's writing is his own attempt to overturn such conceptual structures, and for him the "why" that tempts our inquisitive minds to build those seductive structures is overcome in the name of the "that"—the simple act of beholding, wonder of wonders, that beings are at all![4]

Taking Ignatius's invitation to contemplative practice in silence enables us to retrieve that sense of awe and wonder. He offers detailed directives to consider each and every thing around us—beginning with inanimate objects and going on to plants, then animals, then human beings—and see each of these as a particular case of divine indwelling.

I consider a pebble, among the countless ones I can pick up on the ground. I hold it in my hand and feel its hardness, its bare existence. I consider a shrub in the garden, with its roots buried in the ground, its intertwining branches, its green leaves welcoming the sunlight. I look closely and see a caterpillar inching its way through some leaves, moving now this way, now that way, munching a corner of a green leaf. I turn my gaze to people around me—the jogger passing along the sidewalk in front of the house; the children playing ball in the park nearby; the clerk at the store, helping me check out my groceries; the security guard who greets me as I pass through the door. Each and every one of these persons is a unique gift to the world, just as they are. Their being who they are enriches the world by that much—that is, to an infinite degree more—with each instance. And I, too, am one such individual, a unique gift to the world in my being who I am.

The third point is similar to the second, with an emphasis on the wondrous activity that surrounds each and every thing that exists in the universe. Consider the pebble I mentioned earlier. Our recent scientific discoveries tell us that this hard, bare existence is actually a dynamic movement consisting of subatomic particles that interrelate with one another in the midst of empty space, held together by a mysterious force that gives them mass and form to make up what I perceive as this little pebble in my hand.[5]

Take the same shrub considered earlier, roots buried under the earth from where it draws the water it needs for moisture to nourish its branches and leaves. In your mind's eye, see how natural processes take place as the sun shines upon the leaves and generates energy that enables the chemicals and other elements to interact and make up this living organism that thrives precisely in this interaction with all the elements around it.

Next we consider the caterpillar, moving inch by inch across the leaves and finding its nourishment in its munching. Here we have a new level of a form of life that manifests spontaneity and autonomy. Consider this wormlike figure, crawling and wiggling its way through the leaves; in its own due time, it gradually changes and eventually emerges in glorious form as a butterfly fluttering about from flower to flower.

We turn our gaze to a newly born infant, breathing quietly and contentedly, sleeping in its mother's arms. The very sight of the infant evokes in us a tender sentiment that wants to cuddle and embrace this delicate being, with all the good wishes in our heart that the child may grow up to her full potential as a human being and find the fullness of happiness therein. We imagine the infant as a child of five, playing with other children of the same age at a kindergarten class, in all innocence and simplicity—all laughing and frolicking together.

We imagine her as a teenager, bright-eyed and fluttery as she waits for her date at her first prom. We see her as a young bride throwing her bouquet of flowers to the crowd of young ladies waiting to catch it at her wedding party. We follow her as she becomes a mother herself, bearing and nurturing two children of her own, seeing them through their infancy, childhood, youth, and young adulthood. We now look at her in her advancing years, doting on her grandchildren. In all these stages, we hold in our heart all the wonder and joy, as well as the pains and struggles, and every little detail that makes for the grandeur of life as a human being on this earth.

The fourth point invites us to consider goodness, justice, nobility, honesty, generosity, and such things that make us glad and grateful to be human. As we consider individuals in history who manifested a magnanimous spirit—who lived in ways that embodied goodness, justice, and holiness in their lives—we are uplifted, inspired, and moved to do the same in our own lives.

All four points of contemplation are meant to bring home to each of us, clearly and effectively, that all that we are and all that there is, is so and only so, as a sheer manifestation of the divine Love that permeates everything in this universe and makes everything what it is. And my own being is nothing but a unique and particular manifestation of that same divine Love that also manifests itself in different ways in everything else.

These points are differing angles that intertwine and convey the same basic message in the most direct and intimate way. As I enter into contemplative silence and stay in the depths therein, a voice resounds, taking over all that I am, and flowing out and similarly inundating each and every being that exists in this wide universe: *You are my beloved; with you I am well pleased!* As I look at everything around me—every pebble, every blade of grass, every caterpillar or bird or fish or lion or elephant, and, of course, each and every human being of every age and shape and color and disposition who has ever lived, lives, or will live on this earth—I hear that same voice affirming each and every one with whom I share this be-ing, and in each and every one, in its unique way of being what it is or who it is, the same voice resonates: *You are my beloved; with you I am well pleased!*

The outcome of realizing this is to move me to offer all that I am and all that I have as my grateful response for this Love showered upon me and upon the entirety of creation in abundance, with the same generosity and open-heartedness with which this Love is bestowed: "Take and receive, O Lord, my liberty, my understanding, my will, my all. With your Love and your grace, given to me in abundance, there is nothing else I need." This prayer, widely known as the *Suscipe* (from the first word in Latin, rendered in English as "Take and receive"), is a hallmark of Ignatian spirituality. One who follows the path of Ignatius in contemplative practice through the Spiritual Exercises undergoes an inner transformation in and through the intimate experience of divine Love flowing throughout one's being and through all that exists around us. Soaked in the contemplation of this divine Love, one does not thereby retreat into solitude and silence but rather, empowered by this divine Love, offers oneself as an instrument for the healing of our wounded world.

In sum, right from day one, the Spiritual Exercises provide us with detailed, step-by-step guidelines that lead to this consummate experience of divine Love being poured out unconditionally upon me and the universe. This experience draws forth boundless gratitude in my heart, inspiring as well as empowering me to give back all that I am and all that I have in service to the world, as my way of responding in love to that Love.

Firmly rooted in this experience of unconditional Love, I am able to live my life no longer seeking my own benefit nor worldly ambition, soaked already as I am with all that I can ever want or need. My life is now dedicated to the service of others, seeking the alleviation of their suffering and their full welfare and happiness, as my way of giving back that Love to all beings.[6]

## Notes

[1]Katsuki Sekida, *Two Zen Classics* (New York: Weatherhill, 1977), 375.

[2]*Kuan-yin* (pronounced "kannon" in Japanese) literally means "one who sees the sounds." It is an abbreviated form of *Kuan-shi-yin* in Chinese [one who sees of the sounds of the world] or *Kanzeon* in Japanese. See the chapter titled "Kuan-yin with a Thousand Hands" in Ruben Habito, *Living Zen, Loving God* (Boston: Wisdom Publications, 2005), for a more detailed description of the significance of Kuan-yin in the context of Zen practice.

[3]Sekida, *Two Zen Classics*, 375.

[4]I am indebted to Joseph O'Leary for noting this point in his comments to an earlier draft of this book.

[5]The recent discovery of the Higgs boson, misleadingly referred to as "the God particle," rather than explaining away the fact of materiality, only enhances the sense of awe and wonder at the fact that material things exist.

[6]An oft-repeated theme of Jesuit spirituality is to become "a person for others," adapted also for the wider circle of those following the Ignatian spiritual path—that is, to live as one whose life is no longer seeking one's own goals or ambitions, but one so utterly dedicated to the service of others, empowered by one's experience of unconditional divine Love.

# Conclusion

*Awakened and Transformed in Love:*
*On Being a Contemplative in Action*

The spiritual path opens for us as we begin to pursue questions that cut right through the heart of our very being: "Who am I? What am I here for?" In this book we have looked at the Spiritual Exercises of Ignatius of Loyola, illuminated at various angles from a Zen perspective. In both we have found a rigorous and methodical form of spiritual practice that ushers us through a process of inner transformation. Seen from the point of view of the summit of the Exercises—the Contemplation on Divine Love—we can describe both, each in their own way, as paths of awakening and transformation in love.

We are spurred on in our inward journey as we realize that the way we live our everyday lives leaves much to be desired, bringing us to a state of dissatisfaction and unease. This state of being ill at ease within ourselves is rooted in our living under the sway of our deluded ego that imagines itself to be the center of the universe. In Christian terms, this is to live in sin, a life whereby my thoughts, words, and actions follow the whims and machinations of the ego, the little I-me-mine. Such a way of life causes estrangement from the divine image in which we are made. Our entry into the spiritual path thus calls for us to undertake a stage of purgation or Purification to enable us to set aside those factors in our life that cause or aggravate this state of separation. We looked at the First Week of the Exercises for detailed guidelines in undertaking this stage.

We earnestly seek the Way, looking for guidance about what we are to do, what values we are to uphold, and what attitudes we are to assume. The Spiritual Exercises point us to Jesus as the Way to follow and embody in our own lives. Contemplating the words and deeds of Jesus, and entering into his mind and heart, is the Way to realize our true self. We have considered this as the stage of Illumination that marks the Second Week of the Spiritual Exercises.

As we follow Jesus on the way of the cross and die the Great Death (Third Week), we also rise with him to a New Life (Fourth Week). We discover the risen One in our midst in our daily lives, and we come to appreciate the ordinariness of our lives with a new awakening to its significance. The Eternal manifests itself in this daily life, and we are able to reconcile with all those from whom we thought we were separated. We are now in the stage of Union, the culmination but not the end of our spiritual journey.

The stage of Union is not static but dynamic, opening us to a mystical horizon that grows ever more in depth and intensity.[1] We enter more and more deeply into this mystical life as we engage in the Contemplation on Divine Love that is the summit of the Spiritual Exercises.

But this mysticism is not the kind that stays rapt in ineffability, inaction, and passivity.[2] In this contemplative experience we awaken to none other than the reality of the divine Love itself that permeates the universe. Sitting in stillness we simply bask in the light of this Love, letting it take hold of us and take over our entire life, empowering us to offer our life in loving service to others. The more we give our lives in loving service, the more we experience the intensity of this dynamic Love that underlies, guides, and empowers all our thoughts, words, and actions.

Ignatian mystics are not people who remain cloistered and separated from the rest of the world but instead are those who have awakened to Love; empowered by this Love, they go out and offer themselves at the service of the world for the purpose of healing its woundedness.

Such people are also called "contemplatives in action," an ideal that Ignatius set forth for his followers. They can also be referred to as "engaged mystics," those who cannot remain confined to the cloister but go out into the world and the marketplace (as depicted in the tenth and last of the Zen oxherding pictures), to live out the implications of love.[3]

In the Spiritual Exercises, Ignatius of Loyola has given us a highly methodical, intricately designed approach with many contours and nuances at every turn that nonetheless lead to a starkly simple outcome: the surrender of ourselves in delightful abandon to the divine Love that permeates all, seeking to reunite all to itself, leading us to lives of total surrender to the dictates of this Love.

In a similar way, the Zen path is also described as a "straight path with ninety-nine curves," referring to the simple and direct way of leading us to the heart of the matter, amid the twists and turns of our human lives.[4] The simplicity of the practice is its hallmark. Beyond the preliminary instructions for posture, breathing, and calming the mind, the Zen practitioner is simply told to sit and be still, to plunge right into the stillness and taste what it has to offer.

The Zen tradition offers koans to help untangle the mind from its complex machinations and lead it to that place of ineffable simplicity. These koans are not methodical or systematic by any means. Their power of transforming the practitioner is manifested in the directness, randomness, and spontaneity of the exchange between teacher and student, in the formal encounters undertaken within the context of sitting practice.[5]

We have repeatedly noted that the point of Zen cannot be described in words, as it is a direct transmission outside of Scriptures, conveyed from mind to mind between teacher and student, leading to an experiential event of awakening.[6] It grounds practitioners in a living awareness of the dynamic reality of the present moment. This is not an absorption into a solipsistic realm but rather an opening of a practitioner to the concrete realities of this world of sentient beings with all their pains, sufferings, finitude, and mortality, eliciting a response of loving compassion for all. The figure of Kuan-yin with a thousand hands, reaching out in all directions out of loving compassion for all beings, captures this Zen spirit.

While radically different in so many ways, these two paths of spiritual transformation—the Ignatian Exercises and Zen—also exhibit profound resonances. They both launch seekers on an inward journey through meditative and contemplative practice, allowing them to undergo a process of Purification, Illumination, and Union, and to open to a mystical horizon that empowers human beings to live lives of loving service to others. What occurs for those who follow one of these paths to their ultimate outcome is a transformation in and through the power of Love, received in infinite measure, and poured out in loving service toward healing our wounded earth.

As I note the mutual resonances between these two traditions, I am moved to make two suggestions. First, for those who already have some experience and familiarity with the Spiritual Exercises, taking the path of Zen may enhance and deepen what they are already receiving from the Ignatian tradition of spirituality. Taking the invitation to "just sit and pay attention to your breath" may offer for them a way of cutting through much of the discursive process with which the Exercises tend to be associated, and to be able to enter into a deep contemplative experience more directly and simply. Second, for those already familiar with or engaged in Zen and at home in its stark simplicity, I suggest that they not summarily dismiss as entirely pointless the complex and intricate guidelines that Ignatius prescribed, as the analytic, discursive side of our brain may also have its role in leading us to spiritual heights and depths. Specifically, the exercises of the First Week, and the guidelines for making decisions in life, among others—as well as the contemplative exercises taking imagery from New Testament passages as a starting point—may be of great help to Zen practitioners at different stages of the path, to supplement what is not traditionally offered in this tradition of practice.

I conclude this book with an invitation and a bold statement. If you are at the stage of your life when questions like "Who am I?" "Why am I here?" or "How may I live my best life?" are now nagging at you in a way that you cannot ignore, then by all means do something about it. To repeat an overused quip, "Don't just do something, sit there!"

An invitation is now before you to consider taking up a form of spiritual practice that, if you pursue it seriously and engage in it in a sustained way, will take you through a winding path that may contain surprises for you at every turn. Whether you take the path of Zen or the path of the Spiritual Exercises laid out by Ignatius and his followers—or some other form of practice from another tradition that offers guidelines for an inward journey—pursue it in earnest as a matter of prime importance in your life, and go all the way.

The bold statement is this: If you do take on a path of spiritual practice, and allow it to take you through the stages of Purification, Illumination, and Union, you may open your eyes at some point along the Way and, filled with gratitude, find yourself awakened and transformed by Love.

### Notes

[1]See Harvey Egan, SJ, *The Spiritual Exercises and the Ignatian Mystical Horizon* (St. Louis: Institute of Jesuit Sources, 1976).

[2]I take this term "mysticism" in its simplest sense as deriving from the Greek *muo* [to close the mouth], referring to an experience beyond words and conceptual expression.

[3]See Dorothee Soelle on "engaged mysticism," in *The Silent Cry: Mysticism and Resistance* (New York: Fortress Press, 2001). The Zen oxherding pictures are a series of ten (sometimes eight) illustrations depicting the stages of spiritual path in Zen perspective. The final stage entails a "return to the marketplace"—having attained the heights of mystical experience, a practitioner returns to the ordinariness of daily life and lives in this realm motivated and empowered by compassion for all beings.

[4]See Gregory Shepherd, *The Straight Path with Ninety-Nine Curves: A Zen Journey* (Berkeley, CA: Stonebridge Press, 2013).

[5]See Victor Hori, "The Zen Koan in the Rinzai Curriculum," in *The Koan: Texts and Contexts in Zen Buddhism*, ed. Steven Heine and Dale Wright (New York: Oxford University Press, 2000), 280-315.

[6]This sentence summarizes the so-called Four Marks of Zen. See Ruben Habito, *Healing Breath: Zen for Christians and Buddhists in a Wounded World* (Boston: Wisdom Publications, 2006), chap. 3. This description of Zen thus marks it precisely as a form of spiritual practice that opens one to a mystical horizon, though another angle emphasizes that Zen has nothing to do with the "mystical" (in terms of "esoteric" or "out-of-the-ordinary") but is precisely a way of rediscovering the awe, wonder, and mystery of the ordinary.

# Acknowledgments

This book could not have been written if not for the countless auspicious events and encounters with so many individuals who have graced my life.

I begin by thanking Sr. Rosario Battung and the Good Shepherd Sisters and their staff who hosted the Zen Ignatian retreat I codirected at their retreat house, Maryridge Convent, in Tagaytay City, Philippines, in the spring of 1986, while I was still a Jesuit priest based in Japan. I also thank the ten retreatants, then seminarians of the Mission Society of the Philippines preparing for ordination to the Catholic priesthood. Some of the seminarians who were ordained soon after continue in their priestly ministry, while others have gone on to other things in their life journey.

Since then my own journey has taken me to another land across the ocean, from being a celibate Jesuit priest serving in the Catholic Church in Japan as educator and spiritual director, to my current tasks as faculty member at the Perkins School of Theology, Southern Methodist University, Dallas, Texas, which I assumed in 1989 immediately after leaving the Society of Jesus. Married to Maria Reis Habito and with two college-age sons, Florian and Benjamin, I also serve as guiding teacher of the Maria Kannon Zen Center in Dallas, blessed by a small but vibrant community of Zen practitioners with whom I sit on a regular basis.

My gratitude goes to Nan Lilianne Baker (then Hofheinz), who took it upon herself to transcribe the major part of the tapes of the talks given during that monthlong retreat in Maryridge, Tagaytay, offering helpful written comments and reflections along the margins of her written transcript from her standpoint as a theological student preparing for ministry. I also thank the board of trustees of Stephen Taylor Trust for the Meditation Process, based in St. Paul, Minnesota, for their generous gift that supported the transcription, as well as supporting several retreats that I offered at Osage Monastery (now Osage Forest of Peace), Sand Springs, Oklahoma.

Sr. Pascaline Coff, OSB, then prioress of Osage Monastery, had invited me to offer yearly retreats there for over twenty years since I arrived in Dallas in 1989, and I owe a deep debt of gratitude to her as well as to Sr. Priscilla, Sr. Helen Barrow, and the other members of the community for their welcoming hearts and generous hospitality. I thank Helen Cortes, now also a Zen teacher leading the Tulsa Zen sangha in addition to serving as executive director at Maria Kannon Zen Center, who had served as the monitor and coordinator of those retreats, making sure all the details were in place through countless emails and phone conversations with the Sisters and with the prospective participants so many months in advance each time.

Those retreats at Osage were conducted in a spirit following up on the Zen Ignatian retreat held in the Philippines, and directing and assisting in them gave me an opportunity to learn new things, see new angles, and deepen my appreciation of converging themes in Zen and the Spiritual Exercises of Ignatius of Loyola. The same goes for the retreats I was invited to lead at the Center for Action and Contemplation in Albuquerque, New Mexico, thanks to Fr. Richard Rohr, OFM; Christina Spahn; Kathleen O'Malley; and other directors and staff members of the center. To all those who participated in those retreats over the years, my deepest thanks for walking with me through part of the journey.

I was truly privileged and blessed to have been part of that esteemed band of men, the Society of Jesus, for over two decades. With the guidance of so many Jesuit spiritual masters and mentors through the years, the Ignatian Exercises became a deeply rooted part of my life, even now after many years of having left their company. My ongoing gratitude to the late Fathers James McCaan, Miguel Casals, Charles Wolf, John King, and Thomas Green of the Philippine Province; Thomas Hand, Antonio Evangelista, Hugo Enomiya Lassalle, and William Johnston of the Japan Province; and those who are still with us, Fathers Thomas O'Gorman, Kakichi Kadowaki, and a good number of others with whom I lived in community, who showered upon me their fatherly care, guidance, and wisdom that I continue to treasure among the many great blessings in my life.

To the Jesuits of the Philippine Province, beginning with the late Fathers Benigno Mayo, who challenged me as a perplexed university student and physics major and inspired me to make the leap and enter the Society; Horacio dela Costa who commissioned me to be sent to Japan; and Carlos Abesamis, who remained a friend for life up to his death in 2008; as well as all those with whom I was privileged to live in community in Sacred Heart Novitiate, Loyola House of Studies, and the Jesuit Residence at the Ateneo de Manila University—my deepest gratitude and respect. Included are all who are now in the "XJ Club" like myself, with whom I continue to communicate in an email circle devoted to recalling "the good ol' days" and discussing recent trends. I thank Fr. Catalino Arevalo, who gave the homily at my commissioning rite for the Japan mission at Loyola House of Studies in Quezon City, who now even in his advanced years continues to teach, inspire, and share his wisdom with his Jesuit brethren and the wider community, and Fr. Mario Francisco, president and dean of Loyola House of Studies, for inviting me to offer talks there on occasion.

Special thanks to Fr. Robert Kennedy, SJ, Zen master and dear friend, who visited the Philippines in 1965 as a young priest assigned to Japan, and who told us about the work of the Jesuits there. His talk to us then opened the way for my being sent to Japan a few years later. It was the late Fr. Pedro Arrupe, then superior general of the Jesuits, who sent me on assignment from the Philippines to the Japan Province of the Society of Jesus, for which I remain in a lifelong debt of gratitude.

To all the Jesuits of the Japan Province, especially Fr. Manuel Amoros, my rector at the Kamakura Language School where I spent my first two years learning the language and culture; the late Fr. Thomas Hand, my spiritual director there; Keizo Yamada, with whom I worked closely on justice and peace issues; and all the members of the communities where I lived at Komaba, at SJ House, and at the theologate in Kamishakuji—my deep and heartfelt thanks.

A special tribute of thanksgiving is offered to Fr. Adolfo de Nicolas, SJ, one of my theology professors and spiritual mentors in Japan and now serving the entire Society of Jesus as its superior general based in Rome. To him—and to all those who have been, are, and will be in his company—I dedicate this book with boundless gratitude.

I am indebted to and deeply thank Archbishop Peter Shirayanagi Seichi, who ordained me to the priesthood in Tokyo in 1986; the late Bishop Aloysius Soma Nobuo, with whom I worked closely at the Japanese Bishops' Council for Justice and Peace; Bishop (now Cardinal) Stephen Hamao

Fumio, then of the Yokohama Diocese, who graciously met with me and blessed me as I conveyed to them my departure from Japan; and to Fr. Peter Iwahashi Jun'ichi, then parish priest of Sekimachi Church, where I worked and hung out among the youth of the parish, a good friend and mentor. I thank colleagues at the Nanzan Institute of Religion and Culture, including the late Jan van Bragt, CICM; Fr. Jim Heisig, SVD; and Dr. Paul Swanson, for their support during my transition, and who continue to be friends through the years.

On the Zen side, no words can express my lifelong gratitude to my Zen master, Yamada Kōun Rōshi, who led me by the hand into the intricacies of this spiritual tradition through frequent face-to-face encounters spanning nearly two decades. Mrs. Kazue Yamada—his wife, train seatmate, and close companion in Zen practice and in life through their many years together—opened their household to us who sat in meditation at the San Un Zendō (Zen Hall of the Three Clouds) in Kamakura, Japan, and gave especially those of us who came from other countries her motherly affection and a feeling of being at a home away from home. Many treasured the teaching and guidance of Yamada Kōun Rōshi while he was in robust health, but especially during the last ten months of his life—as he struggled through the pain and suffering of his terminal illness, bedridden and able to do nothing but lie there and live through it—his way of Zen came to be most movingly embodied.

I thank his successors, Kubota Jiun Rōshi and Yamada Ryoun Rōshi, as well as my sisters and brothers in the dharma, especially those of the "first generation" of Sanbō Kyōdan teachers: Sr. Elaine MacInnes, OLM; Joan Rieck; Kathleen Reiley; Anamaria Schluter; Roselyn Stone; Gundula Meyer; David Loy; Sr. Sonia Punzalan; Paul and Katarina Shepherd;

Niklaus Brantschen; Fr. Peter Kopp; AMA Samy; Willigis Jaeger; Uta Dreisbach; Sr. Ludwigis Fabian, OSB; and others, and those already deceased: the late Robert Aitken, Brigitte D'Ortchy, Fr. Victor Löw, Mila Golez, and Silvia Ostertag. We cherish our Zen heritage in a bond of friendship and collegiality forged through years of sitting together at San Un Zendo in Kamakura.

To my friends and fellow members of the American Zen Teachers' Association, a deep bow of gratitude. Through the annual meetings that I have attended sporadically over the years I have learned so much from them and through them, as they witness to the world the many different ways in which an authentic Zen life can be lived.

I am grateful to Natalie Goldberg for her lucid and moving writings that come out of her Zen experience, and especially for her warm welcome received when we visited Santa Fe, thanks to the introduction of dharma brother Henry Shukman.

I thank my coteachers at Maria Kannon Zen Center, Helen Cortes, Valerie Forstman, Lee Ann Nail (now resident teacher at Salem Zen Center in Oregon), Maria Reis Habito, and assistant teacher Joe Benenate, and all Sangha members, for walking closely with me in this ongoing Zen journey. Our Zen community is indebted to so many benefactors named and unnamed, including those who have served as monitors, as coordinators, and as board members of the Zen Center over the years. I especially would like to thank John P. Douglas, who continues to be a good friend and adviser, and John Ockels, who, as we began a Nineteenth Annotation mode of the Spiritual Exercises around the time I was reviewing the transcriptions preparing to write this book, shared with me valuable insights on the First Week and our human condition. To all those with whom I have been graced to sit together in Zen meditation at our Maria Kannon Zen Center in Dallas, as well as in the Zen retreats at the various places I have been invited to offer guidance, I convey my deepest thanks, for they also have been my teachers in many different ways.

I hold a special place in my heart for the Zen communities in my home country, the Philippines. Established in the 1970s by my esteemed and dear dharma sister Elaine MacInnes, OLM, and succeeded by the late Tony Perlas, Sr. Rosario Battung, and Nenates Pineda as teachers, they have continued to flourish over the years. They now have practice centers based in Marikina, Rizal, under the guidance of Elda Paz Perez, Rollie del Rosario, Sr. Rosario Battung, and Carmen Afable; in Bahay Dalangin, in Manila, guided by Sr. Sonia Punzalan, RC, and Fr. Efren Borromeo; in Zamboanga, guided by Sr. Angeles Martinez-Paredes; and in Davao, with Sr. Esperanza Clapano, as Zen teachers. It has been my great joy to reconnect with members of the Philippine sangha in recent years, and I look forward to being with them in Zen retreats in the future.

In the writing of this book I have been given a great gift of time, energy, and wisdom by Paula Sullivan of Seguin, Texas, herself an experienced spiritual guide and director of Ignatian retreats. Paula read through an initial draft and gave me chapter-by-chapter, page-by-page suggestions for polishing the expressions and improving the quality of the language.

I also heartily thank Jessie Dolch, fellow practitioner at Maria Kannon Zen Center, for taking much of her busy time to read an initial draft and for sending me very pointed and insightful comments, raising pertinent questions, and making valuable suggestions about the contents. Thanks to the very specific suggestions and thoughtful remarks of Paula and Jessie, the book in its current form is much less flawed than it would have been otherwise.

I thank fellow Zen teachers Sven Kosnick, Rev. Greg Mayers, and Helen Cortes, along with Jose de Leon, SJ, Jesuit colleague since novitiate days, and Rev. Joseph O'Leary, a friend from Sophia University years, among others, who upon my request sent me very helpful feedback that helped me revise the manuscript.

The raw draft of the transcribed talks that became this book remained on the backburner for many years, until an opportunity to work on it was given to me through a grant from the Perkins Scholarly Outreach Awards Committee. I thank Dean William Lawrence and former Associate Dean Richard Nelson, Elaine Heath, Hugo Magallanes, and former members of this committee who deemed it worthy to approve the grant for this project. I thank my esteemed colleague David Maldonado Jr., Emeritus Professor at Perkins, for his permission to include a moving essay of his on the birth of Jesus. I thank Carolyn Douglas, Mary Ann Marshall, Geneva Hoffman, and others of the Perkins staff for their ever-ready assistance in things big and small, making it easier to get work done.

I am grateful to Jim Keane of Orbis Books, for his able editorial assistance in preparing this book. His having been a Jesuit himself gives me the added joy of working with someone who shares a similar background and experience and who "knows the stuff" I write about in this book. His encouraging attitude provides me the assurance that this book may have something to offer to the wider public. I thank Robert Ellsberg and his fellow editors and staff members at Orbis, including Bill Burrows and Sue Perry, who have now gone on to other things closer to their heart, for all their encouragement and support of my work through the years. Finally, I thank my copyeditor Bob Land and Orbis production coordinator Maria Angelini, who both went through the manuscript meticulously and helped greatly in polishing the final text.

A note of acknowledgment: Biblical citations throughout this book are from the New Revised Standard Version.

# Index

Buddhist diagnosis of,
61–62
features of, 55–61
question of, 52
humility, 119, 131

Ignatius, Saint, 17
defining "spiritual exer-
cises," 24
formed by his times, xiii
life of, ix–x
translating, for a different
culture, 3–5
ignorance, 62, 63, 64
Illumination, xix, xx, , xxii–xxiii,
81, 83, 214, 216
ill will, 62, 64
imagination, 89
incarnation, 95
indifference, 47, 120, 133–34n7
Infinite
path to, xix
pursuit of, 117
infinite Life, awakening to, 203
inner being, connecting with,
25–27
inner peace, 131
insecurity, 58–60, 62, 63
Irenaeus of Lyons, Saint, 43
Islam, 72

Jesuits (Society of Jesus)
beginnings of, x
formation for, 103–4,
126–27
spirituality of, 211n6
undertaking the Spiritual
Exercises, 32n6
work of, x
Jesus. *See also* Christ
ascension of, 194
baptism of, meditation on,

104–6, 137–38, 144–45
birth of, 90–92, 94–95, 97,
98, 144
discernment and, 132–33
dying with all humankind,
186–87
early life of, contemplation
of, 101–2
in Gethsemane, 180–88
of history, 11–12
as human being fully alive,
168
launching his ministry,
143–51
as manifestation of the
Way, 15–16
at one with his True Self,
183
proclaiming the good news,
142–43
returning to Galilee, meditation on, 192–94
suffering of, 172, 174
temptation of, 138, 140–41
temptations of, meditation
on, 114
Jesus Christ. *See* Christ; Jesus
*Jesus Christ Superstar*, 180, 182
Jesus Seminar, 11
Jobs, Steve, 70
John XXIII, xv n4
John Chrysostom, Saint, 86
John Paul II, 57
jubilee year, 149
judo, 158
just sitting, 34–35. *See also*
seated meditation; silence,
sitting in
just this, 35–36, 38–39

Kadowaki, Kakichi, 87
*Kāma Sutra*, 115